TEAMWORK
&
TEAMPLAY
International Edition

50 Team Activities
16 Languages
1 World

D1269847

Dr. Jim Cain

First Printing October 2015

Teamwork & Teamplay International Edition
ISBN 978-0-9882046-3-8

The 16 languages in this volume include:
English, Russian, Chinese, Turkish,
Spanish, Japanese, Mongolian, Italian,
French, Hebrew, Dutch, Greek, Thai,
German, Danish and Portuguese.

For more information about this book, to invite the author to speak at your next event or to purchase additional copies (single or bulk orders), contact the author at:

jimcain@teamworkandteamplay.com

Table of Contents

If you enjoy the content of this book and would like to see a future volume with translations for your country's language (and you are willing to help with those translations) please contact the author at:

jimcain@teamworkandteamplay.com.

Introduction

*"Imagine a world where language is
no longer a barrier to people of every
country working and playing together."*

Dr. Jim Cain

It has been nearly two decades since I wrote the book ***Teamwork & Teamplay*** with my co-author and friend Barry Jolliff. I am pleased that the book has become a valuable reference for teachers, trainers, facilitators and group leaders of all kinds. But what is most surprising to me is the number of books that have been sold internationally over the years, and many of these books are now in countries where English is not the common language.

My first international experience sharing T&T activities was with the staff of LABO, a language and cultural education program in Japan. A few years later, LABO and the Camping Association of Japan translated my Raccoon Circle book into Japanese (my first translation project). A decade later, the Boys Brigade of Hong Kong translated the Raccoon Circle book for the people of China. I enjoyed working with these groups and it was a thrill to hold a copy of a book I had written, presented in a foreign language.

But the ultimate motivation for this book comes from my long association with the

International Camping Fellowship and the increasing number of international camp counselors I meet each year. Anything I can do to assist the wonderful ICF community is indeed my pleasure.

So in 2014 I created the Pangaia Project.* My own personal international diplomacy program. This book you now hold in your hands is the first publication of this project, and I hope there will be many more. After all, there are hundreds of countries (and languages) in our world, and working and playing together is so much better when it becomes teamwork and teamplay!

For this first book of T&T activities with multiple international translations, I have chosen my absolute favorite activities from my personal 'best of the best' list. I have also chosen the activities that require some of the most common and universally available equipment, so that anyone can play, anywhere in the world. I hope you enjoy these activities and the unique collection of international translations presented here. Now you'll be ready for your next playful adventure or powerful training, where ever your travels may take you.

* For information about the Pangaia Project, see pages 215-217 of this book and visit the Teamwork & Teamplay website for additional information at:
www.teamworkandteamplay.com

Teamwork & Teamplay Activities

Icebreakers & Opening Activities

Teambuilding Activities & Challenges

Teamwork & Teamplay Activities

Games Just for Fun

Reviewing Techniques & Closing Activities

For information about the teambuilding equipment featured in this book, see pages 212-214 and visit www.teamworkandteamplay.com and www.training-wheels.com for even more information.

Walking
&
Talking

1 Walking & Talking
An Icebreaker That Moves

Invite everyone to find a partner and link elbows. Next, invite partners to walk together and find three things that they have in common with each other. This combination of walking and talking creates a unique opportunity to build connection between people. Movement creates an active learning environment and appropriate physical connection creates a link between two people that is as much teambonding as teambuilding.

Encourage participants to go beyond convenient similarities such as being the same height or wearing similar shoes. A level one connection is discovering that both partners like to read. A level two connection occurs when they discover they like the same author or have read the same book or visit the same bookstore. The goal of this activity is for each group of partners to identify three, level two connections.

When participants have completed their walk and returned, invite them to share their most unique commonality with everyone in the group.

Link elbows with a partner, walk together and find three things you have in common.

Возьмите друг друга под руку и, прогуливаясь, найдите 3 черты/интереса/ факта, которые вас объединяют.

和一个搭档挽着手，一起边散步边找出三个共同点。

Eşler kol kola yürürken aralarında ortak olan üç şey bulunur.

Con una pareja, entrelazarse codo con codo, caminar juntos conversando y tratar de conseguir tres cosas en común.

2人組になり、腕を組んで┌きます。自由に話しをしながら、お互いの共通点を3つ見つけましょう。

Хамтрагчаа /найзаа/ сугадан алхаж та хоёр гурван ижил төст зүйлээр адилхан байх ёстойг олж мэдэх.

A coppie, prendetevi sottobraccio. Camminate insieme e trovate tre cose che avete in comune.

Joingnez les coudes avec un partenaire, marchez ensemble et trouvez trois choses que vous avez en commun.

שלבו מרפקים עם בן זוג, הסתובבו יחד ומצאו שלושה דברים שיש לכם במשותף.

Loop gearmd met een ander en vind samen drie dingen die je gemeen hebt.

Ενώστε τους αγκώνες σας με έναν συμπαίκτη σας, περπατήστε μαζί και βρείτε τρία πράγματα που έχετε κοινά.

จัดวางข้อศอกให้ติดกันกับเพื่อน, เดินไปด้วยกัน และค้นหาสิง 3 สิงที่เราและเพื่อนมีเหมือนกัน

Finde einen Partner, hake Dich ihm unter, lauft gemeinsam los und findet im Gespräch drei Dinge heraus, die ihr gemeinsam habt.

Tag en partner under armen, gå sammen og find tre ting, som i har til fælles.

Dê o braço a um parceiro, caminhem juntos e procurem três coisas que tenham em comum.

(You can write your own translations here.)

2 The Big Question
An Icebreaking Activity

Each person is given a card with an interesting question written on it. I read my card to my partner and they answer it. My partner asks me the question on their card, and I answer it. We switch cards (which gives me a new question to ask my next partner) and then hold our card high above our head and find a new partner whose card is also in the air, and repeat the process as the activity continues.

The following are examples of Big Questions:

What is the most interesting thing you have ever found? What inspires you? What makes you laugh? What have you lost and then found again? What is the kindest thing you have ever done? If the day was 25 hours long, what would you do with the extra hour? What is your favorite piece of technology? When was the last time you were really surprised? Name three things for which you are thankful. What can you do in your dreams that you cannot do in real life? What is the weirdest thing you have ever eaten? What have you done that makes the world a better place?

You can find over 150 of these great questions on the T&T Training Cards, available from www.training-wheels.com or collect your own questions and write them on index cards.

English Russian Chinese Turkish Spanish Japanese Mongolian Italian

Read the Big Question on your card, invite your partner to answer it. Next, your partner reads the Big Question on their card and you answer it. Then switch cards and find a new partner by raising your card above your head.

Прочтите вопрос на вашей карте, попросите своего партнера ответить на него. Затем вы отвечаете на вопрос по карте партнера. Обменяйтесь картами, поднимите новую карту над головой и таким образом найдите нового партнера.

阅读你卡片上的大问题，邀请你的搭档回答该问题。接着，你的搭档读出他卡片上的问题你来回答。然后，两人互换卡片，通过将卡片举过头顶来找到新的搭档。

Oyunda eşler kartın üstünde yazan Büyük Soruyu birbirine sorarak cevaplar. Daha sonra kartlar değiştirilir ve kart yukarı tutularak yeni eşler bulunur.

Lee la gran pregunta de tu tarjeta, invita a otra persona a contestarla. Esa persona ahora lee su gran pregunta para ser contestada por ti. Al terminar, intercambian tarjetas y se van a buscar otra persona alzando la tarjeta sobre tu cabeza.

2人組で、それぞれが自分の持っているカードに書いてある「質問」を'んで、パ'トナ'に答えてもらいます。そのあと、互いのカードを交換し、それを頭上に'げて、新しいパ'トナ'を探します。（新しいパ'トナ'とまた同じように質問し合います。）

Цаасан дээрх Томоор бичсэн Асуултыг уншаад хамтрагчаа хариулахыг хүсээрэй. Дараа нь таны хамтрагч өөрийн цаасан дээрх Томоор бичсэн Асуултыг уншихад, та түүнд хариулна. Тэгээд хамтрагчтайгаа цаасаа солилцож, цаасаа толгойноосоо дээш өргөн шинэ хамтрагчийг олно.

Leggi la Domanda che c'è sulla tua carta, invita il tuo partner a rispondere. Poi il tuo partner legge la Domanda che c'è sulla sua carta, tu rispondi. A questo punto scambiatevi le carte ed andate in giro a cercare un nuovo partner tenendo la vostra carta sollevata sopra la testa.

Lisez la Grande Question sur votre carte puis invitez votre partenaire à y répondre. Votre partenaire vous posera ensuite la question sur sa carte. Échangez vos cartes et partez à la recherche d'un nouveau partenaire en élevant votre carte au dessus de votre tête.

קראו את השאלה הגדולה על הכרטיס, ובקשו מבן זוג לענות עליה. אח"כ בן הזוג יקרא את השאלה הגדולה על הכרטיס שלו ואתה תענה. החליפו קלפים ביניכם, ומצאו בן זוג חדש ע"י הרמת הכרטיס מעל הראש.

Lees de Grote Vraag op jouw kaart voor aan je partner en nodig hem uit deze te beantwoorden. Vervolgens leest je partner zijn Grote Vraag op zijn kaart voor en geef jij antwoord. Wissel daarna van kaarten en vind een nieuwe partner. Dit doe je door middel van de kaart boven je hoofd te houden.

Διαβάστε την ερώτηση στην κάρτα σας και καλέστε τον συμπαίκτη σας να την απαντήσει. Μετά, ο συμπαίκτης σας διαβάζει την ερώτηση στην κάρτα του και την απαντάτε εσείς. Αλλάξτε κάρτες μεταξύ σας και αναζητήστε νέους συμπαίκτες κρατώντας την κάρτα ψηλά πάνω από το κεφάλι σας.

อ่านคำถามตัวใหญ่บนการ์ด แล้วชวนให้ เพื่อ นตอบ ต่อไปกี้ให้ เพื่อ นอ่าน คำถามตัวใหญ่บนการ์ด ของ เขา แล้ว เราเป็นคนตอบ จากนนั้ กนี้ ลกเปลี่ยน นการ์ด กน และหาเพื่อ นคนใหมไ ปเรือ ยๆโดยชู ราด์ ขนี สูง เหนือศรี ษะ

Finde einen Partner, lies ihm die Frage auf Deiner Karte vor und bitte ihn, die Frage zu beantworten. Danach beantworte im Gegenzug die Frage, die Dir Dein Partner stellt. Abschließend tauscht Eure Fragekarten. Finde einen neuen Interviewpartner, indem Du Deine Karte in die Höhe hältst und einen Teilnehmer zur nächsten Fragerunde einlädst, der ebenfalls seine Karte in die Höhe hält.

Læs det 'store spørgsmål' på kortet og inviter din partner til at svare på det. Derefter læser din partner det 'store spørgsmål' på sit kort og du svarer. Byt kort og find en ny partner ved at holde spørgsmålskortet op over hovedet.

Leia a "Grande Questão" no seu cartão, peça ao seu parceiro que a responda. De seguida, o seu parceiro lê a "Grande Questão" no cartão dele e você responde. Depois troque de cartões e procure um novo parceiro erguendo o cartão acima da sua cabeça.

3 The Story of Your Name
A Get-Acquainted Activity That Builds Respect

Everyone has a story related to their name. Some of us are named after a favorite relative, a close family friend or perhaps even someone famous. Our middle names are significant too. For this activity, invite everyone to share the story of their name. How they came to have it. If they like it or not. Who else has their name. Encourage participants to end with the phrase "please call me.... *their name of choice here*." In this way, everyone will have the opportunity to say how they prefer to be addressed and what is positive about their name.

The underlying and sometimes overlooked potential of this simple activity is the opportunity to create a theme of respect and significance to the name by which people would like to be addressed. In other words, The Story of Your Name is not only a convenient way for people to remember each other's names, but also a way to show respect for every member of the group.

English — Tell the story of how you came to have your full name. Finish by telling the group what name you prefer to be called.

Russian — Расскажите группе о происхождении своего полного имени. В заключение скажите, как лучше всего к вам обращаться.

Chinese — 分享你的名字来由的故事。讲完后告诉大家你希望他们如何称呼你。

Turkish — Gruptan bir kişi isminin ve soyadının hikayesini anlatır. İsminin ne olmasını tercih ettiğini belirterek konuşmayı bitirir.

Spanish — Cuenta al grupo, la historia de cómo y porqué seleccionaron tu nombre completo. Finaliza contando a los demás como quieres que te llamen.

Japanese — 小グル┌プで、自分の名前（姓名）の由┌について話し合います。最後は「自分が仲間からなんと呼ばれたいか」を┌え合って終わります。

Mongolian — Өөрийн овог нэр, та яаж ийм нэртэй болсон тухай түүхээ ярьж, төгсгөлд нь өөрийгөө хэн гэж дуудаж байх нь тохиромжтой болохыг бүлгийнхээ хүмүүст хэлж өгөөрэй.

Italian — Racconta la storia di come mai ti chiami così (Nome e Cognome). Concludi dicendo al gruppo in quale modo preferisci essere chiamato.

Racontez l'histoire de la provenance de votre nom complet. Terminez en partageant avec le groupe par quel nom vous préférez être appelé.

ספר את הסיפור מאחורי שמך המלא. אח"כ ספר לקבוצה באיזה שם אתה מעדיף שיקראו לך.

Vertel de groep het verhaal over hoe jij jouw volledige naam hebt gekregen. Eindig het verhaal door aan te geven hoe jij het liefst genoemd wil worden.

Πείτε την ιστορία για το πώς πήρατε το όνομά σας. Στο τέλος, πείτε στην ομάδα με ποιο όνομα προτιμάτε να σας αποκαλούν.

เล่าเรื่อง งเกยี วกบั ชื่อ จรงิ ของเราว่าเป็นมา อย่างไร ทาไมจงึ มชี ื่อ นี้แลว้ จบดว้ ยการเล่า ใหก้ ลุ่มฟังว่า เรา อยากใหเขาเรยีกเราว่าอะไร

Erzähle die Geschichte, die mit Deinem Namen verbunden ist, z.B. wie Du zu Deinem Namen gekommen bist und was der Name bedeutet. Lass die Gruppe zum Schluss wissen, wie Du angesprochen werden möchtest.

Fortæl hvordan du fik netop dit navn. Afslut med at fortælle hvad du foretrækker at blive kaldt.

Conte a história de como surgiu o seu nome completo. Finalize dizendo ao grupo o nome que prefere ser chamado.

19

4 My Lifeline
An Icebreaking Activity

Groups of four to six people walk together along the lifeline of one member of the group. The line can be a line on the floor, a rope line or any available nearly straight path. As each group walks together, one person shares some of the major milestones (or events) of their life. Obviously, time does not allow for every event in their life, just the significant ones. When they reach the present day position, the person talking also shares one of their goals for the future.

When complete, another person in the group begins at the start of the rope timeline and shares some of the significant events of their life. Continue until all members have had the opportunity to share their life story.

There are three things that each of us uniquely holds - our name, our reputation and our story. This activity provides the opportunity for people to share 'their story.'

For even more games and activities with Raccoon Circles, see *The Revised and Expanded Book of Raccoon Circles* or download the free internet edition of Raccoon Circles at: www.teamworkandteamplay.com

English Tell your group some of the major events or milestones in your life while walking together along a rope line on the floor.

Russian Каким-либо образом обозначьте прямую линию на полу. Пройдя вдоль нее, расскажите группе о самых значимых этапах вашей жизни.

Chinese 和小组成员沿着地上的绳子边走边分享你人生中的一些重大事件或里程碑式的时刻。

Turkish 4-6 kişilik gruplar oluşturulur ve yere bir hat çizilir. Gruplar bu hat boyunca yürürken, gruptan birisi hayatı boyunca yaşadığı önemli olayları grup arkadaşlarına anlatır.

Spanish Mientras caminan una distancia marcada por una cuerda o raya en el suelo, cuéntale a tu grupo alguno de los eventos mas importantes de tu vida.

Japanese 床に置いたロ「プは、過去から未「への「Lifeline」を表します。ロ「プに沿ってみなで「きながら、メンバ「の一人が、これまでの自分の人生の、その時「の重要な出「事「節目について話します。そして"現在"のところまで「きたら、"未「"の目標を語ります。

Mongolian Шалан дээр тавьсан утсан шугамны дагуу хамт алхах зуураа өөрийн амьдралд тохиолдсон зарим нэг чухал үйл явдлын талаар бүлгийнхэндээ ярьж өгнө.

Italian Mentre camminate insieme lungo una corda stesa a terra, racconta al gruppo alcuni degli eventi più importanti o pietre miliari della tua vita.

Dites à votre équipe quelques évènements majeurs de votre vie, tout en marchant ensemble le long d'une corde posée sur le plancher.

ספר לקבוצה חלק מהאירועים הגדולים או ציוני הדרך בחיים שלך,
בזמן שאתם מתקדמים יחד על פס חבל על הרצפה.

Terwijl je samen met je groep langs een koord (een denkbeeldige levenslijn) loopt dat op de grond ligt, vertel je ze een aantal belangrijke gebeurtenissen of mijlpalen in je leven.

Πείτε στην ομάδα κάποια από τα πιο σημαντικά γεγονότα της ζωής σας, ενώ περπατάτε όλοι μαζί κατά μήκος ενός σχοινιού αφημένου στο πάτωμα.

เล่าเรื่อง งของตัว เรา ว่าเคยมี หตุการณ์สาคญ อะไรเกิดใ ขนึ ในชวี ติ เราบา ง หรือ เรื่อ งราวการดาเนินชวี ตี้ ของเราใหเพื่อ นในกลุ่มฟังระหว่างที่เดนิดว้ยกนับนแนวเชือกทวีงอยบู่นพนื

Erzähle Deiner Gruppe von den zentralen Stationen und Ereignissen in Deinem Leben, während ihr gemeinsam an einem Seil am Boden entlang geht, das den Zeitstrahl repräsentiert.

Fortæl om nogle af de store hændelser og milepæle i dit liv, alt imens i går langs et reb på gulvet.

Diga ao seu grupo alguns dos maiores acontecimentos da sua vida enquanto caminham juntos ao longo de uma corda no chão.

5 Over Here!
An Inclusive Opening Activity

Here is an activity that will create an atmosphere of welcome and inclusion for all members of your group. Begin by forming several small groups. Next identify one specific characteristic, such as the tallest person in each group and invite the person who best meets this criteria to step away from the group. When this person leaves the group they become a 'free agent' and other groups can call out, 'over here, over here!' to attract them to join their circle.

There are a few basic rules. You can attract the same person back to your circle. You can invite more than one person to join you. You can go out and recruit if you like, but only to invite folks to join you, not to drag them into your group. Recruitment must be non-contact.

Additional group characteristics include: longest or shortest length of hair, most articles of jewelry, largest shoe size, wearing the most blue or green, number of people living in your house, number of pets, person wearing the coolest watch or cleanest shoes...

Begin in several groups. Invite participants to switch groups based upon criteria (tallest, longest hair, most jewelry…) Shout 'over here' to invite new people to your group.

Начните игру в нескольких небольших группах. Предложите участникам менять группы на базе различных критериев (самые высокие, самые длинные волосы, больше всего ювелирных украшений и т.д.). Зазывайте участников присоединиться к вашей группе «Сюда-сюда».

从几个小组开始。通过不同的标准（如最高的，头发最长的，佩戴首饰最多的等）来邀请参与者转换小组。通过叫喊"来这儿"来邀请他人加入你的小组。

Küçük gruplar oluşturulur. Gruplarda belirli özellikteki kişilerin (en uzun, en uzun saçlı, etc.) grup değiştirmesi ile eksik kalan gruplara yeni kişilerin gelmesi için "buraya" diye bağırılır.

Comience la actividad en varios grupos pequeños. Invite a los participantes a cambiar de grupo basados en diferentes criterios (el mas alto, pelo mas largo, tipo de zapato…) A toda voz invite a nuevas personas a su grupo gritando "aqui aqui".

いくつかの小グループをつくります。グループで相談し、例えば「いちばん背が高い」や「兄弟がいちばん多い」などの件を決め、それにてはまる人は、別のグループに移動しなくてはなりません。った人たちは、「こっちこっち」と大で呼びかけ、移動している人のなかから新しいメンバーを誘います。

Хэд хэдэн жижиг бүлгүүдэд хуваагдаж тоглоомоо эхэлнэ. Оролцогчдыг төрөл бүрийн шалгуураар (хамгийн өндөр, хамгийн урт үстэй, хамгийн их үнэт эдлэлтэй …) бүлгүүдэд хуваагдахыг урина. Өөрийн бүлэгтээ шинэ хүн урихын тулд "энд байна" гэж чангаар хэлнэ.

Si comincia suddivisi in diversi piccoli gruppi. I partecipanti cambiano continuamente gruppi basandosi sui criteri tra i più vari svariati (i più alti, quelli con i capelli più lunghi, chi ha più gioielli, …). Per invitare nuove persone nel tuo gruppo grida "Da questa parte!"

Débuter avec plusieurs petits groupes. Invitez les participants à changer de groupe selon divers critères (le plus grand, cheveux les plus longs, le plus de bijoux…) Criez « par ici » pour inviter de nouvelles personnes à joindre votre groupe.

התחילו במספר קבוצות קטנות. הזמינו משתתפים להחליף קבוצה עפ"י קריטריונים שונים (הכי גבוה, שיער הכי ארוך, הכי הרבה תכשיטים). תצעקו "בוא לכאן" (over here) כדי להזמין אנשים חדשים לקבוצה שלכם.

Start in kleine groepjes. Nodig deelnemers uit om van groep te wisselen op basis van een aantal criteria. (grootste deelnemer, deelnemer met het langste haar, meeste sieraden, enz.) Roep of schreeuw "hier" om nieuwe mensen uit te nodigen in je groep.

Ξεκινήστε με μερικές μικρές ομάδες. Καλέστε τους συμμετέχοντες να αλλάξουν ομάδες ανάλογα με κάποια κριτήρια (ύψος, μήκος μαλλιών, περισσότερα κοσμήματα κλπ) Φωνάξτε «από εδώ!» για να προσελκύσετε καινούρια άτομα στην ομάδα σας.

เริ่ม จากการแบ่งเป็นกลุ่มเล็ก ๆ เรยี กใหผ้ รู้ ว่ มกจิ กรรมเปลยี นก ลุ่มตามคาสงั (เช่น คนตวั สงู ทสี่ ,ุด คน ผมยาวทสี่ ,ุด คนมผี ครอี งประดบั เยอะทสี่ ,ุด เปน็ตน้) โดยตะโกนเรยี กว่า "เราอยนู่ ้"ี เพื่อี หาจานวนสมาชกิ มาเพมิ่ ในกลุ่ม

Beginnt in Kleingruppen. Findet ein Attribut (z.B. der Größte, das längste Haar, der meiste Schmuck,…) und ladet dieses Gruppenmitglied ein, die Gruppe zu tauschen. Gruppen, die ein neues Mitglied brauchen, rufen „Hierher", um auf sich aufmerksam zu machen.

Del jer i små grupper. Inviter deltagere til at skifte gruppe baseret på forskellige kriterier (højest, længste hår, den med flest smykker…) Råb "her over" for at invitere nye til din gruppe.

A actividade começa em vários pequenos grupos. Convide participantes a trocar de grupo baseando-se em vários critérios (os mais altos, os com cabelo mais comprido, os com maior quantidade de acessórios, etc.) Grite "aqui" para convidar novas pessoas para o seu grupo.

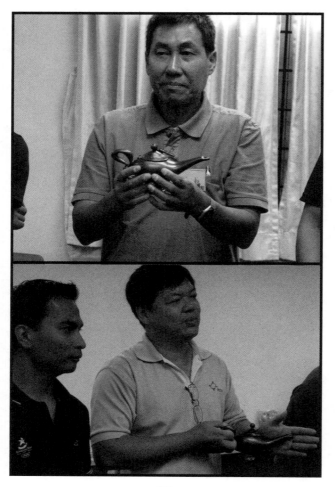

6 The Magic Lamp
A Magical Opening Activity

Legend says that if you find a magic lamp and rub it, a genie will appear and grant you three wishes. The magic lamp in this example is an interesting method of inviting participants to express goals, expectations, hopes, dreams and wishes they have at the beginning of a program.

Begin the Magic Lamp wishing session by rubbing the lamp and then giving an example of an appropriate wish for today's program. When you are finished, offer the lamp to others in the group and invite them to make a wish.

Encourage participants to make wishes for things which can actually happen during the program. Wishes about changing the weather or making tons of money are probably not going to happen during the program, but meeting new people and learning their names probably will!

You can also pass the Magic Lamp around at the end of the program and invite those participants who made a wish at the beginning of the program to comment on whether or not they received their wish during the program.

English Russian Chinese Turkish Spanish Japanese Mongolian Italian

Make a wish for today's program by rubbing the magic lamp. What do you wish for today?

Потрите волшебную лампу и загадайте желание, относящееся к сегодняшней программе. Чего бы вы хотели достичь, узнать или получить именно сегодня?

摩擦神灯并为今天的活动许一个愿。你希望今天收获什么？

Sihirli lambayı ovuştururken günün programı için bir dilek tutulur. Bugün için dileğin nedir?

Sobando la Lámpara Mágica, pide un deseo para el programa de hoy. Qué deseas ocurra el dia de hoy?

魔法のランプをこすって、今日のプログラムについてのお願い事をしましょう。あなたはなにをお願いしますか？

Шидэт дэнлүүг зүлгэж өнөөдрийн хөтөлбөрт оролцох хүслээ шивнэ. Та өнөөдөр юу хүсэж байна?

Esprimi un desiderio per la giornata di oggi strofinando la lampada magica. Cosa desideri per oggi?

Faites un vœu concernant la programmation du jour en frottant la lampe magique. Que souhaitez-vous pour aujourd'hui?

הביעו משאלה בקשר לתכנית של היום ע"י שפשוף מנורת הקסמים. איזו משאלה הבעת ליום הזה?

Doe een wens voor het programma vandaag door over de Magische Lamp te wrijven. Wat wens jij vandaag?

Κάνετε μια ευχή τρίβωντας ένα μαγικό λυχνάρι. Τι εύχεστε για σήμερα;

อธิฐานเพื่อ ขอสั่งที่ อยากได้ร้บัจากโปรแกรมอบรม ของวันนี้โดยการขดัฤตะเกยีงวิเศษ คุณอธิฐานว่า อยากได้อ้ะไร?

Reibe an der magischen Lampe und sprich einen Wunsch für die heutige Veranstaltung aus. Welchen Wunsch hast Du für heute?

Lav et ønske til dagens program ved at gnide på den magiske lampe. Hvad er dit ønske for i dag?

Peça um desejo para o programa de hoje esfregando a lâmpada magica. O que deseja para hoje?

The Story Stretch

7 The Story Stretch
A Warm-Up Activity

This warm-up activity invites each person in the group to tell a story (any theme is possible, such as your favorite activity at summer camp). The story includes both words and actions (*I picked an apple from a tree...* mimic reaching up and picking an apple from a tree). While the leader speaks, each of the other participants in the group duplicates the actions and movements of the leader. After thirty seconds the next person in the group becomes the storyteller and leads the group in a new direction with their own creative contribution to the story and movements. Continue until everyone in the group has had the opportunity to be the leader.

By the time the last person has presented their portion of the story stretch, the entire group is physically warmed up and ready for whatever comes next.

While the primary purpose of this activity is a physical warm-up for participants, there is a secondary opportunity here to discuss leadership, communication and story telling!

One person tells a story with motions, the rest of the group follows the leader. After thirty seconds the next person takes the story and movements in a new direction.

В небольших группах один участник начинает рассказывать некую историю, сопровождая ее богатой мимикой и жестами. Остальные повторяют за ним. Через 30 секунд рассказчик сменяется, и новый участник развивает историю.

每小组选一个人开始讲一个故事并就故事的内容配以相应的动作，小组其他人进行模仿。30秒后换一个人继续讲这个故事并同时配以动作，动作要换一个方向。

Küçük gruplar oluşturulur. Her grupta bir kişi lider olarak, bir yöne doğru yürürken, 30 saniye boyunca mimikler ile bir hikaye veya olay anlatır ve grubun diğer elemanları lideri takip eder. 30 saniye sonrasında gruptan başka bir kişi lider olarak hikayeyi farklı bir yöne doğru yürüyerek devam ettirir. Grupta herkes lider olana kadar oyun devam eder.

Una persona de cada grupo pequeño, cuenta una historia utilizando gestos para cada acción de la historia y el resto del grupo va imitándo los gestos del líder en ese momento. Después de aproximadamente 30 segundos, otra persona del grupo continua la historia y los movimientos en una dirección diferente.

グル┌プの誰か1人がリ┌ダ┌となり、決まったテ┌マ（例えば、キャンプ中の活動でいちばん好きなのは？）について、ジェスチャ┌をつけて話します。┌りの人はそれを見て同じ動作をします。30秒┌ったら、別の人がリ┌ダ┌となり、話題を┌えて┌けます。

Цөөн гишүүнтэй бүлэг тус бүрээс нэг хүн хөдөлгөөнт үйлдэлээр ямар нэгэн түүх яриахад бүлгийн үлдсэн хүмүүс нь ахлагчийг дагана. 30 секунтын дараа дараагийн хүн тэрхүү түүхийг үргэлжүүлэн өөр чигт хөдөлгөөнийг хандуулна.

All'interno di ogni gruppo una persona racconta una storia e la mima con dei gesti, il resto del gruppo imita il leader. Dopo 30 secondi si cambia, la persona successiva continua a raccontare la storia aggiungendo nuovi elementi e nuovi gesti.

Une personne dans chaque petit groupe raconte une histoire en y ajoutant des mimiques, le reste du groupe suit le meneur. Après 30 secondes, la personne suivante prend le relais et poursuit l'histoire, sans oublier les gestes.

אחד מכל קבוצה קטנה מספר סיפור עם תנועות ידיים, והקבוצה מחקה את המנהיג.
אחרי 30 שניות, הבן אדם הבא ממשיך את הסיפור ואת תנועות הידיים לכיוון חדש.

Vorm kleine groepjes. Eén persoon in elke groep vertelt een verhaal en beeldt daarbij ook zijn verhaal uit door middel van bewegingen en gebaren. De rest van de groep doet de leider na. Na een halve minuut is de volgende persoon de leider en vervolgt het verhaal in een nieuwe richting, wederom met bewegingen en gebaren.

Ένας παίκτης από κάθε ομάδα λέει μια ιστορία και ταυτόχρονα την εμπλουτίζει με επεξηγηματικές κινήσεις, ενώ η υπόλοιπη ομάδα μιμείται τις κινήσεις αυτές. Μετά από 30 δευτερόλεπτα ο επόμενος παίκτης συνεχίζει την ιστορία και τις κινήσεις.

สมาชิก คนหนึ่ง จากกลุ่มเล็ก เล่าเรื่อ งประกอบท่าทาง และสมา ชิก ทุกคนทาตามผนู้ า เมอี ครบ 30 วนิาทีเปลยืนใหคันอ่นืออก มาเล่าเรืองประกอบท่าทางโดยใหเคลอ่นืไหวไปในทศิทางอน่ื

Ein Mitglied der kleinen Gruppe beginnt und erzählt eine Geschichte, die er mit Mimik und Gesten untermalt. Die übrigen Gruppenteilnehmer machen die Gesten und Bewegungen nach. Nach 30 Sekunden führt ein anderes Gruppenmitglied die Geschichte in einer anderen Richtung fort, und alle machen jetzt seine Gesten und Bewegungen mit.

En person fra hver gruppe fortæller en historie med bevægelse til. Resten af deltagerne afspejler bevægelserne. Efter 30 sek. fortsætter en anden person historien og nye bevægelser følger.

Em cada pequeno grupo, uma pessoa conta uma história acompanhada por gestos, o resto do grupo segue o líder. Passado 30 segundos, a pessoa seguinte dá continuidade à história e aos movimentos numa nova direcção.

8 Wrapped Around My Finger
An Icebreaking Activity

Begin with one unknotted Raccoon Circle for each group of six people. One person in the group begins wrapping the webbing around their index finger and while doing so tells the group some information about themselves (where they were born, family members, school experiences, childhood pets, favorite foods, etc.) The goal is for this person to continue talking until the webbing is completely wrapped around their finger. When they reach the end, they allow the webbing to unwind and pass it to the next person.

This particular activity provides plenty of time for participants to share information about themselves in a relaxed small group setting. There is a popular theory that for folks that may be a bit shy about speaking in public, the action of wrapping the webbing around their finger occupies that portion of the brain where nervousness occurs. By wrapping and talking at the same time, the speech control center becomes less inhibited and the person talking is typically more relaxed.

The length of a Raccoon Circle allows about one minute of communication, which means you will learn quite a bit more about a person than just their name, occupation and where they live.

Introduce yourself to your group as you wrap the flat rope around your finger. Continue talking until you finish wrapping all the rope.

Наматывая тесьму вокруг своего указательного пальца, расскажите группе о себе. Не заканчивайте рассказ, пока не намотаете всю катушку.

向你的小组成员作自我介绍，边介绍边将扁绳缠绕食指。继续讲直到绳子绕完为止。

Beş metre uzunluğunda bir ip alınır ve bir grup oluşturulur. Gruptan bir kişi ipi işaret parmağı etrafında sarmaya bitirene kadar, gruba kendisini tanıtır.

Mientras enrollas la cinta tubular en tu dedo índice, preséntate a tu grupo. Sigue conversando hasta que termines de enrollar toda la cinta en tu dedo.

自己紹介をしながら、人差し指に平たいロ┌プを┌きつけていきます。そのロ┌プを端まで┌きつけ終わるまで、話を┌けます。

Долоовор хуруугаа туузаар ороох зуураа өөрийгөө бүлгийнхэндээ танилцуул. Туузаа ороож дуустал яриагаа үргэлжлүүл.

Presentati al gruppo e nel frattempo avvolgi la fettuccia intorno al tuo dito indice. Continua a parlare fino a quando non hai finito di arrotolare tutta la corda.

Présentez-vous au groupe en enroulant une corde autour de votre index. Continuez à parler jusqu'à ce que la corde soit complètement enroulée.

הצג את עצמך לקבוצה בזמן שאתה עוטף את החבל השטוח סביב האצבע. המשך לדבר עד שהחבל נגמר.

Stel jezelf voor aan de groep terwijl je een plat koord om je wijsvinger wikkelt. Blijf praten totdat je het hele koord om je vinger hebt gedraaid.

Συστηθείτε στην ομάδα καθώς τυλίγετε ένα κορδόνι γύρω από τον δείκτη σας. Συνεχίστε να μιλάτε μέχρι να τυλίξετε όλο το κορδόνι.

แนะนำตัวให้ มาชกิ ในกลุ่มฟัง โดยเอาเชือ กมาพัน รอบนิ้ว ชี้ ปัดว้ ยในระหว่างทพี ดู อยู่ ให้พู้ดไป เรื ยฯจนกว่าจะพัน จนสุดปลายเชือ ก

Stelle Dich in Deiner Gruppe vor, während Du ein flaches Seil um Deinen Zeigefinger wickelst. Erzähle solange von Dir, bis Du das gesamte Seil aufgewickelt hast.

Præsenter dig selv til gruppen alt imens du vikler et reb om pegefingeren. Tal indtil rebet er rullet helt op.

Apresente-se ao seu grupo enquanto enrola uma corda achatada á volta do seu dedo indicador. Continue a falar até enrolar a corda toda.

Statistical Treasure Hunt

A Mathematical Group Discovery Activity

Add up the score for each of the following categories. The total score is the combined value for EVERY member of your group.

Number of friends on social media.
Your height in inches (or mm).
Number of rooms in your house.
Number of people living in your house.
Number of countries you have visited.
Number of wheels on your primary
transportation device.
Number of books you read each year.
Pairs of athletic shoes you own.
Number of languages you speak.

Total Score = _____

9 Statistical Treasure Hunt
A Mathematical Group Discovery Activity

The challenge of this activity is to add up the total score for each item on the list shown on the previous page for EVERY member of your group. Then compare your group's score with the scores of other groups. Take time during the completion of this activity to discuss some of the quantities with the other members of your group.

There is some math involved, but the real value of this activity is the self disclosure and information sharing that goes on within each group as the final numbers are calculated.

You can find this activity in the T&T Training Cards, available from www.training-wheels.com.

Add up the numbers for your entire group from the treasure hunt list. What is your grand total?

Просуммируйте числа всех участников вашей группы из листа «охотников за сокровищами». Какая общая сумма вашей группы?

从寻宝游戏列表中将整个小组的数字加起来，你们的总数是多少？

Hazine avı listesindeki tüm gruba ait sayılar toplanır. Büyük toplam kaç?

Suma todos los números que consigas de tu grupo una vez completado la lista de la encuesta. Cuál es el gran total?

「探しリストにある項目の「（例えば、持っている靴の「、年「など）を、グル「プのメンバ「全員分、足していきます。全部でいくつになるでしょう？

Эрдэнэсийн эрлийн жагсаалтаас өөрийн бүлгийн бүх хүний тоонуудыг нэмээрэй. Нийт тоо чинь хэд болсон бэ?

Somma i numeri di tutto il gruppo relativamente alle informazioni della lista. Qual è il totale complessivo?

Additionnez les chiffres demandés sur la liste pour votre groupe en entier. Quel est votre grand total?

חברו את המספרים של כל הקבוצה מרשימת חפש את המטמון. מהו הסכום הכולל?

Tel de aantallen van de lijst met schatten van de hele groep. Wat is het eindtotaal?

Προσθέστε τους αριθμούς από τη λίστα χαμένου θησαυρού όλης της ομάδας. Ποιο είναι το τελικό σκορ;

ช่วยกัน บวกตัว เลขจากเกมค้น หาสมบตัิ ในก ลุ่มของเรา เช่น อายุ,เบอรร์ องเทา เพ่อี นบนเฟส บุ้ค เป็น ตน้ ลองดวู าเราบวกเลขไดสุ้้งสุดเท่าไร

Addiert die Zahlen von der Schatzjagdliste für Eure gesamte Gruppe. Wie hoch ist Eure Gesamtsumme?

Tallene fra skattejagten lægges sammen for alle gruppens medlemmer. Hvad er den samlede sum?

Some os números do seu grupo todo da lista da caça ao tesouro. Qual é o seu grande total?

Imaginary Obstacle Course

10 Imaginary Obstacle Course
An Imaginative Warm-Up Activity

This warm-up activity is part creativity and part physical fitness. A volunteer in each small group is selected to begin the activity. Each group will create an imaginary obstacle course, with group members crawling, jumping, running and helping each other through the obstacles they encounter.

After each element, leadership changes and another member of the group describes their obstacle and helps the members of their group navigate over, under, through or around it. In the process, a variety of unusual obstacles can be encountered by the group (climbing a giant marshmallow mountain or running away from a wild animal), creativity and leadership are explored, and the group is warmed-up, energized and ready for the day.

This activity continues until every member of the group has had the opportunity to be the leader.

For other variations of a physical warm-up activity, try The Story Stretch (#7), The Morning Dance Party (#11) and The Leadership Dance (#20) which are also in this book.

Follow your leader as they describe and travel through an imaginary obstacle course. Do what they do. Change leaders after each imaginary obstacle.

Представьте себе, что преодолеваете полосу препятствий. Следуйте за движениями ведущего, который объясняет воображаемое препятствие и вместе со всеми преодолевает его. Меняйте ведущего после прохождения каждого препятствия.

跟随小组组长的描述与动作，共同穿越一个虚构的障碍区。按照他们的动作去做，每跨越一个虚构区中的障碍更换一个组长。

Her grupta bir lider seçilir. Lider hayali bir engelli yürüme parkuru boyunca yürürken, parkuru grup üyelerine tarif eder. Grubun diğer üyeleri liderin yaptıklarını yaparak takip eder. Her hayali engelden sonra lider değiştirilir.

Sigue al líder de tu grupo mientras van describiendo y viajando a través de un campo de obstáculos imaginario. Has lo que el hace. Cambia eventualmente de líder después de atravesar cada campo imaginario.

グル┌プの誰かがリ┌ダ┌となり、想像上の冒┌にメンバ┌を連れていきます。例えば、リ┌ダ┌が（想像上の）木に登ったら他のメンバ┌も登ります。リ┌ダ┌を┌えて┌けましょう。

Дүрслэн харуулсан зохиомол саадыг дуустал нь тэдний тайлбарлах явцаар аялан ахлагчийг дагаж дууриана. Тэдний юу хийснийг яг дууриана. Зохиомол саадыг өөрчлөх бүрт ахлагчийг солино.

Segui il leader del tuo gruppo mentre si muove lungo un immaginario percorso ad ostacoli. Imita quello che fa. Dopo ogni ostacolo immaginario il leader cambia.

Suivez le meneur de votre groupe tandis qu'il décrit et traverse un parcours à obstacles imaginaire. Faites ce qu'il fait. Changez de meneur après chaque obstacle imaginaire.

עקבו אחרי מנהיג הקבוצה שלכם בזמן שהוא מתאר ומתקדם במסלול מכשולים דמיוני. עשו מה שהמנהיג עושה. החליפו מנהיגים אחרי כל מכשול.

Volg de leider van de groep terwijl hij je meeneemt door een denkbeeldige hindernisbaan. Doe wat de leider doet. Verander van leider na elke hindernis.

Ακολουθήστε τον αρχηγό της ομάδας σας καθώς περιγράφει και περπατάει μέσα σε μια φανταστική διαδρομή με εμπόδια. Κάνετε ότι κάνει. Αλλάξτε αρχηγό μετά από λίγο.

ทาท่าตามผนู้ ๅกจิ กรรมของกลุ่ม โดยทที่ ขาจะอธปิ ๅยถงึ การเอาชนะอุปสรรคบางอยา งทที่ ขา จนิ ตนาการขนี้ มา ทาตามไปเรอื่ ยๆโดยเปลยี นสมาชกิ คนอ่นี ออกมาเล่าถงึ อุปสรรคในจนิ ตนาการ

Folge dem Leiter Eurer Gruppe, der sich auf einen imaginären Hindernislauf begibt. Mache alles nach, was er vormacht. Wechselt den Leiter nach jedem imaginären Hindernis.

Leg "kongens efterfølger", alt imens lederen beskriver en usynlig forhindringsbane. Gør som lederen gør. Skift leder efter hver bane.

Imite o líder do seu grupo enquanto ele descreve e viaja através de um campo de obstáculos imaginário. Faça o que ele faz. Troque de líderes depois de cada obstáculo imaginário.

11 The Morning Dance Party
A Warm-Up Activity With Music

The dance party is a great morning warm-up activity. One person in each circle of twenty or more people begins dancing a simple basic movement to the music being played and everyone else in the group does the same thing. After a few seconds, the leader points to the person on their left, who becomes the next dance instructor of the group and contributes their own movements (which everyone follows). The leadership continues to move around the circle until everyone has had the opportunity to be the leader.

For the ICF International Camping Conference in Antalya, I was asked to lead a one hour 'speed dating' session at the start of the conference. With people attending from over thirty countries, language would indeed be a challenge, so I opted to incorporate a series of mixer dances, so that people could meet & greet and dance together. Music is truly a universal language and so is dancing.

English

In a large circle, each person takes a turn as dance leader for the group while dance music plays. Everyone follows the leader.

Russian

В большом кругу под танцевальную музыку каждый участник по очереди показывает свое танцевальное движение. Все повторяют за ведущим.

Chinese

在一个大圆圈中，每个人轮流随着音乐领舞。其他人照做。

Turkish

Büyük bir daire oluşturun. Dairede bir kişi dans lideri seçilir. Bir şarkı boyunca grubun diğer elemanları dans liderini takip ederek dans eder. Gruptaki her kes sırasıyla dans liderliği yapar.

Spanish

Mientras va sonando la música, en un gran círculo, cada participante toma un turno para dirigir el baile para el resto del grupo. Los demás siguen la coreografía del líder.

Japanese

大きな円をつくります。ダンスの音「が流れたら、リ「ダ「が簡「なダンスを踊り、みんなで「似します。リ「ダ「は次「に交代していきます。

Mongolian

Хөгжмийн аянд том тойрогт орсон хүн бүр ээлж ээлжээр бүжгийг ахалж бүжиглэнэ. Бусад нь ахлагчаа дагаж бүжиглэнэ.

Italian

In un ampio cerchio, ogni persona a turno guida le danze al ritmo di una musica da ballo. Tutti seguono ed imitano i movimenti di chi guida.

En grand cercle, chaque personne mène tour à tour la danse pendant que la musique joue. Tout le monde imite le meneur.

במעגל גדול, כל אחד בתורו הוא מנהיג הריקוד עבור הקבוצה בזמן שמוזיקת הריקודים מנגנת. כולם עוקבים אחרי המנהיג.

In een grote kring neemt ieder persoon op zijn beurt de leiding terwijl er dansmuziek speelt. Iedereen volgt de leider.

Σε έναν μεγάλο κύκλο, κάθε παίκτης με τη σειρά του χορεύει, ενώ οι άλλοι παίκτες τον μιμούνται.

ยนี ลอ้ มวงกนั เป็นวงกลมใหญ่ ใหแ้ ต่ละคนสลบั สบั เปลยี นกนั ออกมาเป็นผนู้ ำท่าเต้น ประกอบดนตรี สมาชกิคนอ่นื่ๆเต้นตามท่าทางของผน้ำ

Stellt Euch in einem großen Kreis auf. Jeder Teilnehmer übernimmt abwechselnd die Aufgabe des Vortänzers, während Tanzmusik spielt. Alle anderen machen dem Vortänzer nach, was dieser vortanzt.

Alle står i en stor cirkel. Man skiftes til at lede dansen i gruppen, alt imens musikken spiller. Alle følger 'danselederen'.

Num grande círculo, cada pessoa tem a vez de ser o líder de dança do grupo enquanto música toca. Todos seguem o líder.

12 Bull Ring

A Teambuilding Activity for Large Groups

A Bull Ring is a metal ring with 12 strings attached to it, useful for transporting a small ball (such as a golf ball or tennis ball). Participants are asked to hold only the ends of a string. Challenges include passing through a doorway, lifting the ball up and down and the final challenge, having three groups simultaneously touch their tennis balls together at the same time. This final challenge requires teamwork, communication, leadership and timing! Or you can create a candelabra and see if multiple groups can place their tennis balls on the stand at the same time.

For variety you can invite your group to choose which ball they wish to transport (small, lighter balls are easier, while bigger, heavier balls are more challenging). On a hot summer day, you can replace a ball with an ice cube, but you'll need to move fast or the ice cube will melt!

You can make a Bull Ring from a metal ring or you can try a 3-D version made from a plastic tube.

Practice carrying a ball with the Bull Ring and then bring together three groups so that the three balls simultaneously touch each other.

Потренируйтесь переносить теннисный мяч с помощью «бычьего кольца», а затем попробуйте сделать так, чтобы мячи трех групп одновременно коснулись друг друга.

练习用鼻环来搬运一个网球，然后让三组人将三个网球同时接触。

Üç grup oluşturulur ve gruplar bir birlerinden ayrı olarak Bull Ring ile tenis topu taşır. Daha sonra üç tenis topunun aynı anda bir birine dokunması için üç grup bir araya getirilir.

Practica cargando una pelota de tennis con el "Bull Ring" (Argolla de Toro) y luego acerca a los tres grupos de manera que las tres pelotas de tennis estén en contacto simultáneamente.

12本のヒモが結びつけられたリングにテニスボ「ルをのせて、落とさず運べるよう練習します。最後は3グル「プがそれぞれ持ち上げたボ「ルを同時に接「させてみましょう。

Бухын цагирагаар ширээний теннисний бөмбөгийг тогтоогоод гурван бүлгийг тус бүрийн теннисний бөмбөгийг нэгэн зэрэг нийлүүлэх багийн тоглоом.

Allenatevi a trasportare una pallina da tennis con il Bull Ring, poi mettete insieme tre gruppi e fate in modo che le tre palline da tennis si tocchino simultaneamente tra loro.

Pratiquez-vous à transporter une balle de tennis avec l'anneau et les ficelles. Joignez ensuite trois sous-groupes et tentez de faire toucher simultanément les trois balles de tennis.

התאמנו בנשיאת כדור טניס בעזרת הטבעת (bull ring), ואז קרבו שלוש קבוצות יחד כדי ששלושת הכדורים יגעו זה בזה באותו זמן.

Oefen met de Bull Ring door een tennisbal een kleine afstand te dragen. Dan, breng drie groepen samen op zo'n manier, dat de drie tennisballen elkaar tegelijk raken.

Κάνετε εξάσκηση να μεταφέρετε μια μπάλα του τένις με το Bull Ring και μετά ενώστε τρεις ομάδες, ώστε τα τρία μπαλάκια να ακουμπούν το ένα στο άλλο ταυτόχρονα.

ฝึกเลยๆ งลกู เทนนิสใหท้ รงตวั อยปู่ นห่วงกลม จากน นั้ ใหท้งั้ สามกลุ่มมาช่วยกนั เลยๆ งลกู เทนนิสๆของ ตนเอง ใหค้อยๆเคล่อืนมาอย่ชูดิรวมกนัตรงกลางห่วงทงัสามลกู

Übt, einen Tennisball mittels eines Bull Rings zu transportieren. Bringt dann drei Gruppen zusammen, so dass sich die drei transportierten Tennisbälle gleichzeitig berühren.

Der øves i at bære en tennisbold med en "bull ring". Få de tre grupper til at arbejde sammen, så de tre tennisbolde samtidig rører hinanden.

Pratique carregar uma bola de ténis com o "Bull Ring" e de seguida junte três grupos de forma a que as três bolas de ténis se toquem em simultâneo.

13 The Fishhook
A Teambuilding Activity

The Fishhook tool is a wooden block with metal hooks, supported by 12 strings. Players pull on the strings to maneuver the block and hooks to perform tasks, such as stacking several wooden blocks (that also have eyescrews and hooks on them) or the more difficult task of picking up and setting down a mousetrap without triggering it.

I created this teambuilding activity as part of a character education program. I connected twelve strings to a block of wood with metal hooks attached to it. I also found several wooden fish at my local craft store and attached a metal eyescrew to each. Then I invited my team to go fishing. On the back of each fish was a character word which the team discovered when they caught the fish. For a higher level of challenge, ask your team to pick up a set mouse trap, without setting it off. A significant challenge that most groups can accomplish.

English Russian Chinese Turkish Spanish Japanese Mongolian Italian

Use the Fishhook to stack three blocks or pick up (and set down) a mousetrap.

Используя рыболовный крючок, поставьте три блока друг на друга или поднимите и опустите мышеловку так, чтобы она не захлопнулась.

使用鱼钩来堆积三块木头或拾起（然后卸下）一个捕鼠器。

Olta kullanarak 3 kutu üst üste konulur veya yerde duran fare kapanları toplanır (ve yere indirilir).

Utiliza un anzuelo para colocar tres tacos uno encima del otro o recoge (y luego suelta) una trampa de raton.

12本のヒモを結びつけた釣り針をあやつって、3つの木のブロックを積み重ねたり、ネズミ捕りを持ち上げて設置したりしてみましょう。

Загасны дэгээ ашиглан гурван шоог өрөх юмуу эсвэл хулганы хавхны дэгээг авах/тавих сорилт.

Usa l'Amo da Pesca per accatastare tre blocchi o sollevare (e poi appoggiare a terra) una trappola per topi.

Utilisez l'hameçon afin d'empiler trois blocs ou ramassez puis déposez une trappe à souris.

השתמשו בוו (fishhook) כדי לעשות ערימה של שלוש קוביות או להרים (ולהניח) מלכודת עכברים.

Gebruik de Fishhook (vishaak) om drie blokken bovenop elkaar te zeten of om een muizenval op te pakken (en weer neer te zetten).

Χρησιμοποιήστε το Fishhook για να βάλετε τρία τεμάχια το ένα πάνω στο άλλο ή να ανεβάσετε (και να κατεβάσετε) μια ποντικοπαγίδα.

ใช้ตะขอเบด็ ตกปลามาเป็นเครอื งมออ ยกแท่งไม้มาเร ยี งกนั 3 แท่ง หรอื หวี ขนึ เพ่อ ปลดลอ็ คกบั ดกั หนู โดยไมให้กบัดกัดดีตวั

Nutzt den „Fischhaken", um damit drei Holzblöcke aufeinander zu stapeln oder eine gespannte Mausefalle vom Boden aufzuheben (und wieder abzusetzen), ohne dass sie zuschnappt.

Brug "fiskeblokken" til at stable tre blokke eller at løfte og sænke en musefælde.

Use o " Fishhook" para empilhar três blocos ou para levantar (e baixar) uma ratoeira.

14 Peteca
A Physical Activity That Explores Changing Rules

This Brazilian game is typically played like a hand version of badminton, but for our purposes, we will play it in a small circle.

The goal is for a circle of ten people to keep the peteca in the air for 21 hits. The true challenge comes when the rules for keeping the Peteca in the air change with each round.

Play begins with players using both of their hands. Then using only their non-dominant hand. Then both hands but only standing on one foot. Medium level challenges include: turning a 360 circle (spin) after each hit, clapping three times after hitting the Peteca, touching the ground after hitting the Peteca, or high fiving someone after hitting the Peteca. Higher level challenges include: rotating the circle of people clockwise while hitting the Peteca or singing a song while playing.

In groups of ten people, keep the Peteca in the air using: two hands, one hand, standing on one foot, moving in a circle, while singing.

В группах по 10 человек, удерживайте петеку в воздухе, используя две руки/одну руку/стоя на одной ноге/делая оборот вокруг себя после удара/напевая.

以10人为一组，分别通过使用双手、单手、单脚站立、边唱边转圈的方式，让Peteca始终保持在空中。

10 kişilik gruplar oluşturulur. Gruplar iki ellerini kullanarak, tek ellerini kullanarak, tek ayak üstünde şarkı söyleyerek, daire etrafında yürürken Peteka havada tutulur.

En grupos de 10 personas, mantener la Peteca en el aire usando: dos manos, una mano, parado sobre un pié, moviéndose en círculo, silvando.

グルｰプの10人で協力して、"ペテカ"を落とさないように手で打ち上げｰけます。ｰ手で、片手で、片足立ちで、円の中を動き回りながら、歌いながら、など、ルｰルをｰえたり加えたりしてｰけます。

Оролцогчдыг тус бүрдээ арван хүнтэй баг болгон хуваана. Дуу дуулах, тойргоор алхах, нэг хөл дээрээ зогсох зуур хоёр гар, нэг гараараа Петекаг агаарт тогтоон барина.

In gruppi da dieci persone, tenere in aria la Peteca usando: due mani, una mano, stando su un piede solo, muovendosi in cerchio, cantando.

En groupes de dix personnes, gardez le Peteca dans les airs en utilisant : deux mains, une main, debout sur une jambe, en tournant en cercle, en chantant.

בקבוצות של 10 אנשים, השאירו את ה-Peteca באוויר ע"י שימוש ב: שתי ידיים, יד אחת, בזמן עמידה על רגל אחת, בזמן שזזים במעגל, בזמן ששרים.

In groepen van tien personen, houdt de Peteca in de lucht met behulp van: twee handen, één hand, staand op één voet, terwijl men in een rondje loopt en terwijl men zingt.

Σε ομάδες των δέκα ατόμων, κρατήστε το Peteca στο αέρα με τους εξής τρόπους: με δύο χέρια, με ένα χέρι, κουτσό στο ένα πόδι, κινούμενοι σε κύκλο, τραγουδώντας.

จัด กลุ่มขนึ มา 10 คน โดยซ่วยกนั ทาใหสั ก ขนไก่ลอยตูวิ อยใ นอาฑาศตลอดเวลาอยา ใหต่ กพนี อาจใช้ มอืสองขาง หรอืมอืขางเดยีวยนีขาวเดยีวและเคล่อืนไหวไปรอบๆเปน็ วงกลมพรอัมกบัรอัองเพลงไปดวัย

Haltet in einer Gruppe von etwa 10 Teilnehmern einen Peteca in der Luft. Variiert dabei: Schlagen mit zwei Händen, nur mit einer Hand, auf einem Fuß stehend, im Kreis drehen, dabei singen.

I grupper på ti personer få Petecaen til at blive i luften ved at benytte: to hænder, en hånd, ved at stå på et ben, dreje omkring sig selv alt imens I synger.

Em grupos de dez pessoas, mantenha a Peteca no ar usando: duas mãos, uma mão, num só pé, movendo-se num círculo, cantando.

63

15 Magic Carpet
A Teambuilding & Goal Setting Challenge

A Magic Carpet is any plastic tarp about 6 feet (2 meters) square. 8-12 people stand on this tarp and are then challenged to turn the tarp over (to the other side) without lifting people up and without touching the floor or ground below the magic carpet. Multiple groups working together at the same time may lead to some interesting collaborative solutions.

For additional possibilities, invite participants to set a goal for themselves and write this goal on a piece of masking tape and fasten it to one side of the Magic Carpet. Then turn the tarp over and write down some of the barriers or obstacles to achieving these goals. Encourage participants to share their goals and barriers out loud with the other members of their group. Begin the activity on the barrier side of the Magic Carpet and challenge the group to reach the goal side.

Turn over the Magic Carpet without lifting people up or touching the ground.

Переверните «волшебный ковер» оборотной стороной, не поднимая стоящих на нем участников игры и не касаясь пола.

翻转魔毯，同时既不能将人举起来也不能碰触地面。

8-12 kişi sihirli halı üstünde yerlerini alır. Sihirli halı üstündekiler yere dokunmadan, havaya zıplamadan sihirli halıyı ters çevirir.

Voltea la alfombra mágica sin levantar a ninguna persona o tocar el suelo.

グル「プ全員が"魔法のカ「ペット"に「ります。誰かを持ち上げたり、誰かが地面に足をついたりしないようにして、カ「ペットを裏返します。

Хүмүүсийг дээш үсрэлгүйгээр эсвэл газар хүргэлгүйгээр шидэт хивсийг хөмрөх.

Girate il Tappeto Magico senza sollevare persone o toccare terra.

66

Retournez le tapis magique sans soulever personne ni toucher le sol.

הפכו את מרבד הקסמים בלי להרים אנשים או לגעת ברצפה.

Draai de Magic Carpet (het magisch tapijt) om zonder iemand op te beuren of dat men de grond raakt.

Γυρίστε ανάποδα το μαγικό χαλί χωρίς να σηκώσετε ανθρώπους και χωρίς να αγγίξετε το έδαφος.

พยายามพลิก ตลบกลบั ข๋ งพรมวิ ศษ โดยไมย่ กพรมใหล้ อยขนิ และไมใ ห้คนทยี นิ บนพรม แตะพนิ

Wendet den Magischen Teppich, ohne dass Teilnehmer angehoben werden oder den Boden berühren.

Vend det "magiske tæppe" om på den modsatte side uden at løfte deltagerne eller at røre jorden/gulvet.

Virem o "Tapete Mágico" ao contrário sem levantar ninguém ou tocar no chão.

16 Back Writing
A Communication Activity

Teams of five people sit in a straight line. The person in back is presented with a simple image (written on a piece of paper) and asked to communicate this information to the person in front of them, using just their finger to write the image on the back of this person. The image continues to move forward in the line of people until it reaches the front and the final person draws the image (as they know it) on an index card. The final drawing is then compared to the original image. A fun communication activity.

English

Using your finger, write a picture on the back of the person sitting in front of you. Pass the picture forward until the final person in line draws the picture on an index card. Compare the final drawing to the original picture.

Russian

Указательным пальцем нарисуйте на спине следующего игрока картинку, полученную от ведущего. Продолжайте таким образом «передавать» образ от одного игрока к другому. Когда последний игрок получит информацию, сравните начальную картинку с итоговой.

Chinese

使用食指，在你前面人的后背上画一个图。以这种方式将这个图传递到队列最前面并由最后一个人将这幅图画到一张索引卡上。和原始图画比较。

Turkish

5 kişilik takımlar oluşturulur ve takımdaki kişiler arka arkaya sıralanır. En arkadaki kişiye üzerinde bir şekil olan kağıt gösterilir ve kağıt üzerindeki şekli önündeki kişinin sırtına işaret parmağı ile çizmesi istenir. Oyun, sırtına şekil çizilen kişinin önündekinin sırtına şekli çizmesiyle devam eder. Sıranın en önündeki kişi sırtına çizilen şekli bir kağıda çizer. Son olarak, en öndeki kişinin kağıda çizdiği şekil ile en arkadaki kişiye verilen kağıttaki şekil karşılaştırılır.

Spanish

Usando su dedo índice, escribir un dibujo en la espalda de la persona sentada delante de ti. Siga pasando la imágen hacia adelante hasta que la última persona de cada fila dibuja la imágen en una hoja o tarjeta blanca. Comparen el dibujo final con la imágen original.

Japanese

人差し指で前の人の背中に┌を描きます。描かれた┌をまたその前の人の背中に、と次┌に送っていきます。最後の人がその┌をカ┌ドに描いたら、最初の┌と見比べてみましょう。

Mongolian

Оролцогчдыг цуваа болгон суулгана. Цувааны хамгийн сүүлд сууж байгаа гишүүн урдаа суугаа найзынхаа нуруун дээр долоовор хуруугаараа зураг зурна. Энэ зургийг цааш дамжуулсаар цувааны хамгийн урд сууж байгаа гишүүн самбар дээр гарч тэр зургийг зурна. Сүүлчийн зургийг эх зурагтай харьцуулна.

Italian

Usando il dito indice, fai un disegno sulla schiena della persona seduta davanti a te. Nel gruppo continuate a passare il disegno in avanti fino a quando il primo della della fila riporta il disegno su un cartoncino. Paragonate poi il disegno sul cartoncino con l'originale.

En utilisant votre index, dessinez une image sur le dos de la personne assise devant vous. Celle-ci reproduira le dessin vers les personnes de l'avant jusqu'à ce que la dernière personne en ligne dessine l'image sur un carton. Comparez le dessin à l'image originale.

השתמש באצבע וציר ציור על הגב של הבן אדם שיושב לפניך. המשיכו להעביר את התמונה קדימה עד שהבן אדם האחרון בתור מצייר את הציור על כרטיס. השוו את הציור הסופי לציור המקורי.

Teken met je wijsvinger een afbeelding op de rug van de persoon die voor je zit. Die persoon tekent de afbeelding op de rug van degene die voor hem zit. Ga zo door tot aan de persoon die vooraan in de rij zit. Die persoon tekent de afbeelding op een kaart. Vergelijk dan de kaart met de originele afbeelding.

Χρησιμοποιώντας τον δείκτη σας, ζωγραφίστε μια εικόνα στην πλάτη του συμπαίκτη που βρίσκεται μπροστά σας. Εκείνος θα ζωγραφίσει την ίδια εικόνα στον μπροστινό του, μέχρι ο τελευταίος στη σειρά να ζωγραφίσει την εικόνα σε ένα χαρτί. Συγκρίνετε την τελική ζωγραφιά με την αρχική.

ใช้นิ้วชี้ วาดภาพบนหลัง ของเพื่อ นที่นี่ นั่ง อยู่ข้ า งหน้าของเรา วาดต่อกันไปเรื่อ ยๆจนถึ คนหน้าสุด จากนั้นให้ค้นทอียหู่น้ำสุด ของแถวาดภาพบนหลังบนการ์ดแล้วเอ้ามาเปรียบเทียบกับการ์ดคา สงว่าได้ภ้าพเหมอือนหรอือ แตกต่างกันอยางไร

Male mit dem Zeigefinger ein Bild auf den Rücken des Teilnehmers, der vor Dir sitzt. Dieser wiederum zeichnet das gleiche Bild auf den Rücken seines Vordermanns. Der letzte Teilnehmer in der Reihe malt das Bild auf eine Karteikarte. Vergleicht nun die Zeichnung auf der Karte mit dem ursprünglichen Bild.

Med pegefingeren tegnes et billede på ryggen af personen foran dig. Bliv ved med at give tegningen videre indtil den sidste i rækken tegner billedet på et stykke papir. Sammenlign tegningen med det originale billede.

Usando os vossos dedos indicadores, desenhem uma figura nas costas da pessoa sentada á sua frente. Continuem a passar a figura para a frente até que a pessoa do fim da linha a desenhe num papel. Comparem o desenho final ao original.

17 Shoe Toss
A Goal Setting Activity

Each person takes off one shoe, and then sets a goal for themselves by throwing the shoe in front of them. The shoe can travel a short distance, or a long one or anything in between. Next, each person closes their eyes and walks towards their shoe. The goal is to reach down and touch their shoe without bumping into it or searching about for it, thereby achieving their goal.

The opportunity here is a discussion about setting goals for ourselves. Do we set challenging goals? Are our goals too easy? Too difficult? Impossible? What are we doing to achieve our goals?

Each person throws one shoe in front of themselves, then walks to recover the shoe with their eyes closed. Was their shoe goal too easy, too difficult, or just right?

Каждый игрок снимает один ботинок и бросает перед собой. Затем, закрыв глаза, идет подобрать свой ботинок. Была ли задача найти ботинок слишком легкой/слишком сложной или как раз по силам?

每个人将一只鞋扔到自己前面。然后，闭眼走到鞋边并捡起来。这个任务是否太容易还是刚刚好？

Oyundaki kişiler ayakkabılarından birini çıkarır ve ileri fırlatır. Daha sonra gözlerini bir bez ile bağlarlar. Gözleri bağlı şekilde ayakkabıyı bulmaya çalışırlar. Ayakkabıyı bulmak çok mu kolaydı yoksa çok mu zordu?

Cada persona lanza un zapato delante de si. Luego camina con los ojos cerrados, para recuperar su zapato. Fué facil, dificil o sencillo conseguir el zapato?

グループのそれぞれが片方の靴を前方に投げ飛ばします。そして、目を閉じて、自分の靴を回しにいきましょう。間違わずにできたかな？

Хүн бүр өрөөсөн гутлаа урдаа шидээд нүдээ анин алхаж очоод гутлаа авна. Энэ даалгавар хэтэрхий хялбар, хэтэрхий хэцүү эсвэл боломжийн байсан уу?

Ognuno lancia una scarpa davanti a sè. Poi cammina per recuperare la scarpa con gli occhi chiusi. L'obiettivo-scarpa è stato troppo facile, troppo difficile o ben calibrato?

74

Chaque personne lance un soulier devant elle, puis marche les yeux fermés pour retrouver son soulier. Est-ce que leur objectif de soulier était trop facile, trop difficile ou juste correct?

כל אחד זורק נעל אחת קדימה, ואז הולך להרים את הנעל בעיניים עצומות. האם המטרה הייתה קלה מדי, קשה מדי, או בדיוק מתאימה?

Ieder persoon gooit één schoen voor zich uit. Loop dan met je ogen dicht naar de schoen toe om hem op te halen. Was het doel (de schoen dus) te makkelijk te bereiken, te moeilijk of juist precies goed?

Κάθε παίκτης πετάει ένα παπούτσι μπροστά του. Μετά περπατάει με τα μάτια κλειστά για να το βρει. Ήταν πολύ εύκολο, πολύ δύσκολο ή ακριβώς ό,τι έπρεπε;

ทุกคนโยนรองเท้า ของตนเอง 1 ข้า งออกไปด้า นหน้า แล้ว เดินิ หลับ ตาออกไปหารองเทา ของตนเอง ลองดซู วิ า การ หารองเทา นนั้ มนั า ย หรอื ยาก หรอื ไมเ ท่าไหร่

Jeder Teilnehmer wirft einen seiner Schuhe vor sich auf den Boden. Mit geschlossenen Augen läuft er nun auf den Schuh zu und bückt sich dann (immer noch mit geschlossenen Augen), um ihn aufzuheben, ohne nochmal danach zu suchen. War das „Schuhziel", das sich der Teilnehmer gesetzt hat, zu einfach, zu schwer oder genau richtig?

Hver deltager smider deres ene sko frem foran sig. Går efterfølgende med lukkede øjne ud for at hente deres sko. Var deres mål for nemt, for svært eller helt rigtigt?

Cada pessoa atira um sapato para a sua frente. Depois vai buscá-lo com os olhos fechados. Foi o seu sapato um objectivo demasiado fácil, demasiado difícil, ou perfeito?

French Hebrew Dutch Greek Thai German Danish Portuguese Notes

For a higher level of challenge, try this activity
using two Raccoon Circles that are the same color.

18 Missing Link
A Consensus Building Activity

Good judgement comes from experience,
and experience comes from bad judgement.

Two Raccoon Circles (of different colors) are placed on the ground. It should not be obvious whether these two loops are LINKED or UNLINKED. The initial challenge is for individuals to decide whether the two circles are linked or unlinked, without touching them.

Invite participants to stand on the left side if they believe the loops are linked and on the right side if they believe the loops are unlinked. Next have one person from each side take a partner from the opposite side and discuss their decision until one partner changes their mind. Finally, when everyone is ready, pull the loops so the group can discover whether they are linked or unlinked.

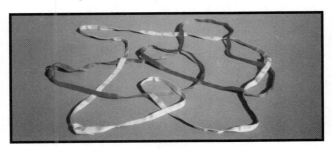

Decide if the two rope circles are linked (connected) or unlinked (not connected).

Придите к общему мнению, соединены или разъединены два канатных круга.

判断两条绳圈是否相连。

Gruplar yerde bulunan iki ip halkasının birbirine bağlı veya bağlı olmadığına karar verir.

Decidan si dos cuerdas en circulo estan entrelazadas (conectadas) o desenlazdas (desconectadas)?

色違いの2本のロ「プの輪が、床にぐちゃっと重ねて「げてあります。ロ「プに「らずに、この2つの輪がつながっているかいないか、相談して考えてみましょう。

Хоёр олсон тойргууд холбогдсон эсвэл холбогдоогүйг тодорхойл.

Decidete se i due anelli di corda si intrecciano (sono connessi) o non si intrecciano (non sono connessi).

78

Décidez si les deux cercles de corde sont noués ou distincts.

החליטו האם שני עיגולי החבל מחוברים או לא מחוברים.

Besluit of de twee cirkels aan elkaar verbonden zijn of niet.

Αποφασίστε αν οι δύο κύκλοι από σκοινί είναι συνδεδεμένοι ή όχι.

ลองเดาดูว่าวงเชือ กทวี วงอย่จู ะถูกทาให้เช่อื ม ต่อกนั หรอื ไมเช่อื มต่อกนั

Versucht (ohne die Seile zu berühren) heraus zu bekommen, ob die zwei Seile miteinander verbunden sind oder voneinander unabhängig auf dem Boden liegen.

Gæt om de to reb hænger sammen (forbundet) eller ikke har forbindelse med hinanden (ikke forbundet).

Decidam se as duas cordas estão interligadas ou não.

19 Not Knots
A Consensus Building Activity

In this activity, a 'rope doodle' is constructed and the group is challenged to decide whether the rope will create a KNOT (please stand to the left side) or NOT A KNOT (move to the right side) when the ends of the rope are pulled apart. The oportunity here is to provide tools a group can use when they cannot achieve consensus. Typically, about half of the group thinks the doodle will form a knot and the other half a straight line. Ask participants to partner with a person that has a different viewpoint and try to achieve consensus with them. By considering a different possibility, participants learn to value alternative points of view. The good news is, for this consensus building activity, one of the two people in the group is correct! Then choose a side together, Knot or Not a Knot.

At this point, it is likely that there will still not be a complete consensus within the group. Prior to pulling the ends of the rope, let the members of the group know that you will pull the rope, slowly, and they can change sides at any time during the unraveling of the knot doodle as more information becomes available. Not Knots also provides the opportunity to fail forward. Learning from our mistakes improves our future decision making process.

Decide if the rope will form a knot or a straight line when the ends are pulled apart.

Придите к общему мнению, образует ли канат узел, если потянуть за его концы.

判断绳子两端拉开时是否会打结。

Uçlar çekildiğinde ipte düğüm oluşup oluşmayacağına karar verilir.

Decidan si al halar las puntas de la cuerda, se forma un nudo o no.

床にぐちゃっと┌げてあるロ┌プ、端と端を引っ張って伸ばしたら、結び目ができるかできないか、相談して考えてみましょう。

Олсны хоёр үзүүрийг татах үед олс зангилаа үүсгэж байна уу эсвэл шулуун байна уу гэдгийг тодорхойлох.

Decidete se, tirando le due estremità in direzioni opposte, la corda formerà un nodo o una linea retta.

Décidez si la corde formera un nœud ou un ligne droite lorsque les bouts seront tirés.

החליטו האם החבל ייצור קשר או שורה ישרה כאשר ימשכו בקצוות.

Besluit of het koord een knoop zal vormen of een rechte lijn wanneer de eindpunten uit elkaar getrokken worden.

Αποφασίστε αν το σκοινί θα κάνει κόμπο ή μια ευθεία γραμμή όταν τραβηχτούν οι άκρες του.

ลองเดาดูว่าเมื่อ ดึง ปลายทั้ง สองข้า งออกจนสุด วง เชือ กจะผูก เป็นเงือ น หรือ คลายออกเป็นเส้น ตรง

Versucht (ohne die Seile zu berühren) heraus zu bekommen, ob das Seil einen Knoten hat oder eine gerade Linie ergibt, wenn man es an beiden Enden auseinander ziehen würde.

Gæt om rebet danner en knude eller en lige linje, når der bliver trukket i enderne af rebet.

Decidam se a corda irá formar um nó ou uma linha direita quando as duas pontas forem puxadas.

The Leadership Dance

20 The Leadership Dance
Exploring Leadership With Music & Dance

For this high energy leadership activity each person in the group is invited to be the dance instructor/leader for one song. Leaders do not know the song in advance, so whatever music plays - they lead. When the music changes, the next person in the group becomes the leader.

Start by forming groups of nine people. Next, invite the members of the group to count off (one through nine) and to remember their number.

You'll need a collection of nine different songs for this activity. Familiar, energetic songs are perfect, especially if they have a definite beat or rhythm. For each song, you'll need about 45-60 seconds (roughly 1 minute) of music. Be sure to call out the number of the next leader at the beginning of each song.

At the completion of the activity, discuss which leadership styles worked best, who were the most effective leaders, what techniques made people a successful leader and other leadership issues as experienced by the group.

In small groups, each person becomes the dance leader for one song.

В небольших группах каждый участник ведет по одной песне. Остальные повторяют движения за ним.

在小组中，每个人轮流为一首歌领舞。

Küçük gruplar halinde herkes bir şarkı boyunca dans lideri olur.

En grupos pequeños, cada persona se convierte en el líder coreográfico para cada canción.

小グル「プで、1人1曲、ダンスのリ「ダ「に なりましょう。誰のダンスがイイかな？

Цөөн хүнтэй бүлэг дэх хүн бүр нэг дууны аянд бүжгийг ахалж бүжиглэнэ.

In piccoli gruppi, ogni persona guida le danze per il tempo di una canzone.

En petits groupes, chaque personne mène la danse le temps d'une chanson.

בקבוצות קטנות, כל אחד נהיה מוביל הריקוד לשיר אחד.

In kleine groepjes wordt ieder persoon voor één liedje de dansleider.

Σε μικρές ομάδες κάθε παίκτης γίνεται ο αρχηγός του χορού για ένα τραγούδι.

จับ กลุ่มเล็ก ๆ ให้แ ต่ละคนสบั เปลยี นกนั ออกมาเป็นผนู้ าเตน้ กนั คนละเพลง

Jedes Gruppenmitglied wird für die Dauer eines Liedes der Leiter und gibt die Tanzbewegungen für die Gruppe vor.

I små grupper bliver en person på skift danseleder af en sang.

Em pequenos grupos, cada pessoa se torna líder da dança para uma música.

The Bobsled Team

21 The Bobsled Team
A Fast-Paced Teambuilding Activity

When it comes to high performing teams, the four members of a world-class bobsled team may be the best example ever. This activity explores that level of high performance and teamwork. Begin with teams of four people standing in a line (like a train), hands on the shoulders of the person in front of you. Then introduce the following three commands:

Change - the person at the front of the bobsled team (#1) moves to the rear (#4) of the same bobsled.
Switch - team member number two (#2) trades places with team member number three (#3).
Rotate - everyone individually turns 180 degrees.

In round one, invite teams to listen and follow several of your commands. Then give teams two minutes to practice the change, switch and rotate commands on their own. In round two, stack more commands together (change-change-switch-rotate). In round three (the championship round) add the command **"Loose Caboose"** - where everyone scatters and must quickly become part of a new bobsled team of four.

After this activity, discuss how practice and teamwork can improve the performance of a team.

English

Teams of four people practice these bobsled movements: Change (#1 becomes #4), Switch (#2 and #3 change places), Rotate (everyone turns 180 degrees), Loose Caboose (everyone scatters and forms a new team of four people).

Russian

Разбейтесь на «бобслеи-четверки». И потренируйте следующие команды: поменялись (#1 становится #4), махнулись (#2 и #3 меняются местами), повернулись (все разворачиваются на 180 градусов) и свободный бобслей (все рассыпаются в поисках новой четверки).

Chinese

四人一组练习大雪橇运动：变换（第1个人换到第4个人的位置），转换（第2和第3个人改变位置），旋转（每人180度旋转），解散（小组解散后形成一个新的四人小组）

Turkish

Bu kızak hareketlerini dört kişilik gruplar uygularlar: değişim (1. Kişi 4. Kişi olur), Değiş-tokuş (2. kişi ve 3. Kişi yer değiştirir), Çevir (herkes 180 derece döner), Başıboş Vagon (herkes dağılır ve yeni bir dört kişilik grup kurar).

Spanish

En equipos de 4, practiquen estos "bobsled' movimientos: Cambio (el #1 se pasa al puesto del #4), Rotan (el #2 y el #3 cambian de puestos) Giran (todo giran sobre su eje 180 grados) Loose Caboose o Loco Furgon (todos se mezclan para formar nuevos equipos de 4)

Japanese

4人でボブスレ「チ「ムになり、かけ「に合わせて次の動きをします。「チェンジ：1人目と4人目が交代」「スイッチ：2人目と3人目が交代」「回「：全員が180度回「」「ル「スカブ「ス（切り離し）：バラバラになって、新たな4人組をつくる」

Mongolian

Дөрвөн хүний бүрэлдэхүүнтэй баг эдгээр бобслей хөдөлгөөнийг хийнэ: Өөрчлөх (#1 нь #4 болох), Солигдох (#2 ба #3 байраа сольно), Эргэлдэх (хүн бүр 180 градус эргэлдэнэ), сул Caboose (бүгд тараад дахин дөрвөн хүний бүрэлдэхүүнтэй баг болж цуглана).

Italian

Gruppi di quattro persone fanno pratica con questi movimenti tipici del Bob a Quattro: Change (#1 diventa #4), Switch (#2 e #3 si scambiano di posto), Rotate (tutti ruotano di 180 gradi), Loose Caboose (tutti si disperdono e vanno a formare nuovi gruppi di quattro persone).

En équipe de quatre personnes, pratiquez ces mouvements de bobsleigh : Changement (#1 devient #4), Transfert (#2 et #3 échangent de place), Rotation (tout le monde tourne de 180 degrés), Déraillement (tout le monde se disperse pour reformer des groupes de quatre personnes).

קבוצות של ארבעה אנשים מתאמנים בתנועות המזחלת הבאות: לשנות (change) = מספר 1 נהיה מספר 4, להחליף (switch) = מספר 2 ומספר 3 מחליפים מקומות, להסתובב (rotate) = כולם מסתובבים 180 מעלות, קרון משוחרר (Loose caboose) = כולם מתפזרים ויוצרים קבוצות חדשות של ארבעה אנשים.

In teams van vier personen, oefen deze bobslee manoeuvres: Ruil (persoon #1 wordt #4), Wissel (#2 ruilt van plaats met #3), Omdraaien (iedereen draait zich 180 graden om), Loose Caboose (iedereen verspreidt zich en vormt een nieuw team van vier personen.

Σε ομάδες των τεσσάρων ατόμων κάντε εξάσκηση τις εξής κινήσεις ελκήθρου: μεταβολή (το #1 γίνεται #4), περιστροφή (το #2 και το #3 αλλάζουν θέσεις), μεταβολή (όλοι στρίβουν 180ο), μπάχαλο (όλοι σκορπίζονται και σχηματίζουν νέες τετράδες).

จัด ทีมี 4 คนตั้ง แถวตอนเรียง งหนึ่ง เล่นเกมเคลื่อ นไหวอสิ ระ: โดยสลับ คนที่ 1 กับ คนที่ 4, สลับ คนที่ 2 กับคนที่3,แล้วให้ทุกคนกลบัหลงัหนั180องศาทงั แถว,จากนนั้กระจายตวัออกจากกนัเพอื่ไปตงั้แถว4คนกบัเพอื่นคน อ่นืๆต่อไป

Vier Teilnehmer bilden die Mannschaft eines Viererbobs und führen folgende Bewegungen aus: Auf den Befehl „change" geht der erste nach hinten (#1 wird #4), „switch" (#2 und #3 tauschen die Plätze), „rotate" (jeder dreht sich um 180 Grad), „loose caboose" (alle Mannschaften mischen sich neu und bilden neue Viererbobs.

I grupper på fire øves følgende bobslæde bevægelser. Skift: (nr. 1 skifter plads med nr. 4) Switch: (nr. 2 og nr. 3 skifter plads) Roter: (alle drejer sig 180 grader) Loose Caboose: (alle danner nye hold af fire personer).

Equipas de quatro pessoas praticam estes movimentos de andar de trenó: "Muda" (#1 torna-se #4), "Troca" (#2 e #3 trocam de lugares), "Roda" (todos rodam 180 graus), "Loose Caboose" (todos se espalham e formam uma nova equipa de quatro pessoas).

22 Sunny Side Up
A Teambuilding Challenge

While the task of this teambuilding activity is very simple, it will challenge even the best team. Begin with a group of six to ten people holding the perimeter of a large plastic tarp about waist high. Place a tennis ball on the tarp in the center. Challenge the group to toss the ball into the air (using the tarp to launch the ball), turn over the tarp (180 degrees) and successfully catch the ball on the way back down.

If you wish to encourage a group to do some problem solving and planning before trying this activity, remove the tennis ball and ask them to practice the movements of the toss, turn and catch without the ball until they believe they have a technique that will be successful. Then, when they are confident, give them a ball and see what happens.

You can also try this task with a balloon (it moves much slower which can be especially useful if young children are playing) or a beach ball or a stuffed toy animal (or a rubber chicken).

Using a tarp, toss a ball into the air, turn over the tarp, catch the ball with the tarp on the way back down.

Используя брезент, подбросьте мяч в воздух, переверните брезент обратной стороной и поймайте мяч.

使用一块油布，将一个球投向空中，翻转油布并接到落下来的球。

Bir muşamba kullanarak tenis topunu havaya atın, o havadayken muşambayı ters çevirin ve topu tekrar muşambayla yakalayın.

Usando una lona, lanza una pelota la aire, debes voltear la lona para atajar la pelota.

全員でタ「プの「をつかみ、「ん中に置いたボ「ルを「ませて高く上げます。ボ「ルが落ちてくる前にタ「プを裏返し、キャッチします。

Берзент ашиглан бөмбөгийг дээш шидэж, берзентээ эргүүлэн бөмбөгийг буцаж унах замд нь барьж авна.

Usando un telo, lanciate la pallina in aria, capovolgete il telo, con il telo riprendete al volo la pallina che sta ricadendo.

En utilisant une toile, faites voler une balle dans les airs, retournez la toile, et rattrapez la balle qui retombe avec la toile.

בעזרת משטח, זורקים את כדור באוויר, הופכים את המשטח, ותופסים את הכדור עם המשטח בדרכו מטה.

Gooi de bal met het zeildoek in de lucht. Draai het zeildoek om en vang de bal met het zeildoek als de bal weer naar beneden komt.

χρησιμοποιώντας έναν μουσαμά, πετάξτε μια μπάλα στον αέρα, γυρίστε τον μουσαμά ανάποδα, πιάστε την μπάλα με τον μουσαμά στην κάθοδό της.

ใหช้ ว่ ยกนั จบั มุมของผนี ผ้า ใบหรูอี ผนี พลาสตกิ โยนลกุ เทนนิสขนี้ ในอากาศ พลกิ กลบั ขา งผนี พลาสฺตกิ พรอ้มๆ กนัแลว้พยายามเอาผนีพลาสตกิรบัลกูเทนนิสใหไ้ด้

Benutzt eine Plastikplane, um einen Ball in die Höhe zu schleudern, dreht die Plane um (oben nach unten) und fangt den Ball wieder mit der Plane auf.

Brug en presenning, smid en bold i luften ved brug af presenningen. Vend presenningen og fang bolden når den er på vej ned.

Usando uma lona, atirem uma bola ao ar, e tentem apanha-la com o outro lado da lona.

23 Blind Trust Drive
A Trust Building Activity

Begin with partners (teams of two people) in an open space, with one partner standing behind the other. The front 'driver' holds onto an imaginary steering wheel and closes their eyes. The 'backseat driver,' eyes open, places their hands on the driver's shoulders and tells them, "I will take care of you." The front driver controls the speed, while the rear person provides information and direction (a human GPS system), avoiding collisions with other drivers and fixed objects. After a few minutes, the front driver opens their eyes and provides the following feedback to their GPS person:

> *What was good about their technique?*
> *What could they do to be even better?*

Next, the two participants exchange roles, repeat the activity, and conduct another feedback session.

This is an excellent activity for beginning a more in-depth trust sequence. Be sure to have plenty of supervision and a safe, open space. If you happen to see a few 'fender-benders' or collisions, your group may require additional work before they are prepared to take care of each other. If you observe caution, carefulness and no accidents, your group is probably ready to proceed to another trust building activity. For a higher level, try this activity with no physical contact between the driver and GPS unit, only verbal communication.

The front partner steers an imaginary car with their eyes closed. The rear partner is the GPS unit and talks to the driver to help them travel safely.

Игрок впереди с закрытыми глазами рулит воображаемой машиной. Игрок сзади говорит с водителем, как GPS, и помогает ему ехать безопасно.

前面的搭档闭着眼睛驾驶一辆虚拟汽车。后面的搭档作为导航告诉驾驶员方向，帮助他们安全驾驶。

Öndeki takım elemanı gözleri kapalı bir şekilde hayali bir araç kullanır. Arkadaki takım elemanı GPS cihazı olur ve önündeki sürücünün güvenli bir şekilde yolculuk edebilmesine yardımcı olmak için onunla konuşur.

La pareja que esta al frente maneja un carrito imaginario con los ojos cerrados. La pareja que va atrás, es su GPS y dirige al conductor para viajar de manera segura.

2人組で運┌手とカ┌ナビの役を決めます。運┌手役は目を閉じ、カ┌ナビの指示に┌って、安全に運┌をします。

Урд сууж байгаа хамтрагч нүдээ аниад зохиомол автомашиныг жолоодох дүр үзүүлнэ. Арын суудалд сууж байгаа хамтрагч GPS-ын үүргийг гүйцэтгэн урд сууж байгаа жолоочийг чиглүүлэн аюулгүй зорчиход тусална.

Il partner davanti tiene gli occhi chiusi e fa finta di guidare un'auto immaginaria. Il partner dietro è il GPS e parla con l'autista per aiutarlo a guidare in modo sicuro.

Le partenaire à l'avant conduit une voiture imaginaire avec les yeux fermés. Le partenaire à l'arrière imite un appareil GPS et parle au conducteur avant afin de l'aider à se déplacer de manière sécuritaire.

בן הזוג הקדמי מנווט מכונית דמיונית עם עיניים עצומות. בן הזוג האחורי הוא הGPS ומדבר אל הנהג הקדמי כדי לנסוע בבטחה.

Met zijn ogen dicht, bestuurt de persoon die vooraan staat een denkbeeldige auto. De partner die achter hem staat is de GPS en praat tegen de bestuurder om hem veilig te laten reizen.

Ο μπροστινός κάθε ζευγαριού οδηγεί ένα φανταστικό αυτοκίνητο με τα μάτια κλειστά. Αυτός που στέκεται πίσω του είναι το GPS και μιλάει στον οδηγό για να τον βοηθήσει να οδηγήσει με ασφάλεια.

สมมุติ ให้ พ่อ นคนหน้าสุดทาหน้าที่ เป็นคนหลุบ ตาควบคุมพวงมาลัย ขบั รถ เพ่อ นคนทอี ยขู่ า งหลุงั ทา หน้าที่เป็นGPSคอยบอกทศิทา งการเคล่อืนไหวและคอยบอกให้ไปตามทางทปีลอดภยัไม่ชนกบัคนอ่นีี

Zwei Teilnehmer stehen hintereinander, der Hintermann hat seine Hände auf den Schultern des Vordermanns. Der Vordermann steuert ein imaginäres Auto mit geschlossenen Augen. Der Hintermann agiert als Navigationssystem. Während sich die beiden durch den Raum bewegen, gibt der Hintermann dem Vordermann Anweisungen, damit dieser sicher durch den Verkehr kommt.

Den forreste partner styrer en usynlig bil med lukkede øjne. Den bagerste partner er GPS'en, som taler til bilisten, for at hjælpe vedkommende med sikker kørsel.

O parceiro da frente guia um carro imaginário com os olhos fechados. O parceiro de trás é como um dispositivo de "GPS" e fala com o condutor para este viajar com segurança.

24 Jump Rope Challenge
A Teambuilding Activity

Ten pieces of rope, from 1 to 10 feet (30 to 300 cm) in length are presented to a group of 8-30 people. Beginning with the shortest rope (1 foot long), each rope must be jumped three consecutive times before the next longer rope can be jumped. The total time required to jump all the ropes is the score. Time begins on the first jump of the shortest rope and concludes with the third jump of the longest rope.

There are three roles in this activity. Participants can be a 'jumper' or a 'rope twirler' or a timer. Some ropes are long enough for a single person to twirl and jump by themselves. The shortest ropes will require two people to twirl the rope and another person to jump it. During each turn, the rope must circumnavigate the jumper (go completely around them).

A score time of 45 seconds or less is good. A score time of 30 seconds or less is world class! Encourage participants to find a job that suits their own abilities and that helps the team as a whole.

English Teams work together to jump 10 ropes (of different lengths) 3 times each, as fast as they can.

Russian Командам нужно как можно быстрее по три раза перепрыгнуть через 10 веревок, каждая из которых разной длины.

Chinese 团队协作共同跳完10根绳子。每根长度不同，每根绳子跳三次，用他们最快的速度完成。

Turkish Takımlar beraberce, hepsi farklı uzunluklarda olan on ipten her birinin üzerinden üç kere olacak şekilde, ellerinden geldiğince hızlı biçimde atlarlar.

Spanish Los grupos trabajan en equipo para saltar 10 cuerdas de saltar (con diferentes longitudes, tres veces cada una lo mas rápido que puedan.

Japanese 10種類の長さの違うロープで跳びをします。3回連で跳べたら、次のロープに移り、10種類すべてを跳び終わる速さを競います。

Mongolian Багууд өөр өөр урттай арван дээсэн дээгүүр аль болох хурдан гурван удаа үсрэх даалгаварыг гүйцэтгэнэ.

Italian Il gruppo deve trovare il modo per saltare dieci corde (ognuna di lunghezza differente) per tre volte ciascuna, il più velocemente possibile.

Les équipes travaillent ensemble afin de sauter trois fois par-dessus dix cordes (toutes de longueurs différentes), aussi vite qu'elles le peuvent.

קבוצות עובדות יחד לקפוץ בעשרה חבלים (כל אחד באורך שונה) שלוש פעמים כל אחד, הכי מהר שאפשר.

Teams werken samen door touwtje te springen met tien touwen van verschillende lengtes. Elk team doet dit drie keer en zo snel mogelijk.

Οι ομάδες συνεργάζονται για να παίξουν σκοινάκι με δέκα σκοινάκια διαφορετικού μήκους, τρεις φορές στο κάθε ένα, όσο πιο γρήγορα μπορούν.

ทั้ง ทมี ช่วยกนัน กระโดดขา้ มเุชอื กทลี ะเสน้ ซงึ มคี วามยาว ต่างกนั ตอ้ งกระโดดขา มใหไ ด้ 3 ครงั ต่อเุชอื ก แต่ละเสน้ พยายามกระโดดใหพ้รอ้มกนัและเรว็ทสีุดจนขา้มครบทงั้10เสน้

Das Team soll 10 unterschiedlich lange Seile jeweils drei Mal so schnell wie möglich überspringen. Dabei wird vom kürzesten Seil zum längsten Seil gearbeitet. Das nächst längere Seil darf erst dann übersprungen werden, wenn das kürzere Seil 3 Mal hintereinander übersprungen wurde.

Gruppen arbejder sammen om at hoppe over 10 forskellige tov (i forskellige længder). Alle skal hoppe igennem 3 gange, så hurtig som muligt.

Equipas trabalham em conjunto para saltar por cima de dez cordas (cada uma com comprimentos diferentes) três vezes cada um, o mais rápido que conseguirem.

103

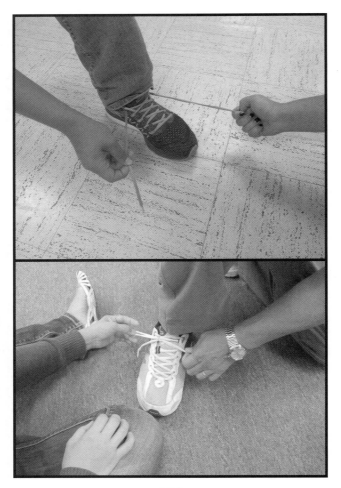

25 Shoelaces

A Teambuilding Challenge for Two People

Here is a simple teambuilding challenge for partners. At least one person must have shoes with laces that tie.

Ask one person in each group of two to untie the bow of the laces on their shoes. Next, with one partner supplying one hand and the other partner also supplying just one hand, ask them to work together to re-tie the shoe laces.

After this first attempt, ask them to repeat the process, this time using their non-dominant hand. Finally, ask them to repeat the process again, but this time with their eyes closed.

Partners will need communication, problem solving skills and teamwork to succeed in this task.

English Two people work together to tie a shoelace, using just one hand from each person.

Russian Двое партнеров, используя правую руку одного и левую руку другого, стараются завязать шнурки.

Chinese 两人共同完成系鞋带，每人只能用一只手。

Turkish İki kişinin ikisi beraberce ve fakat sadece bir ellerini kullanarak bir ayakkabı bağcığını bağlamaya çalışırlar.

Spanish Dos personas trabajan juntas para amarrar la trenza de un zapato, usando unicamente una mano cada uno.

Japanese 2人組になって、それぞれ片方ずつの手を使い靴ひもを結びます。

Mongolian Хоёр хүн хамтарч өрөөсөн гараараа нэгнийхээ гутлын үдээсийг үднэ.

Italian Due persone devono riuscire ad allacciare una stringa da scarpe, usando soltanto una mano ciascuna.

Deux personnes travaillent ensemble afin de boucler un lacet, en utilisant chacun une seule main.

שני אנשים עובדים יחד לקשור שרוך, אך כל אחד
משתמש רק ביד אחת.

Twee mensen gebruiken ieder één hand om samen een schoenveter vast te maken.

Δύο παίκτες συνεργάζονται για να δέσουν τα κορδόνια ενός παπουτσιού, χρησιμοποιώντας ένα χέρι ο κάθε ένας.

จบั ค่กู บั เพ่อื นฺ แลว้ ช่วยกนั ผกู เชอื กรองเทา้ ดว้ ยมอื คนละขา้ ง ช่วยกนั ผกู ใหส้ าเรจ็

Zwei Partner binden gemeinsam die Schnürsenkel eines Schuhes. Dabei darf jeder nur eine seiner Hände verwenden.

To personer arbejder sammen om at binde et snørebånd ved kun at bruge en hånd hver.

Duas pessoas trabalham em conjunto para atarem um atacador usando apenas uma mão um do outro.

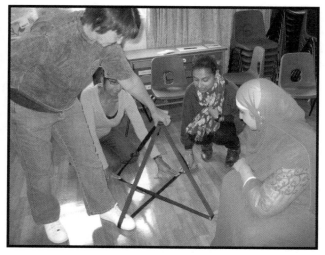

26 Shape Up
A Teambuilding Activity for Young Children

While holding a knotted Raccoon Circle, small groups of people create various shapes as directed by the facilitator. Shapes can include: The letter E, a jet airplane, a tree, a house, the number 4, a four-legged farm animal. More complicated, three-dimensional shapes, such as a cube or a pyramid, can be used for high performing groups.

   While Shape Up is primarily an activity for younger children, teamwork, communication and leadership can each be explored with this activity for group members of any age. And, for an even higher level of challenge, you can try this activity blindfolded (without sight)!

English Russian Chinese Turkish Spanish Japanese Mongolian Italian

Small groups work together to form numbers, letters, shapes and objects with a rope circle.

В маленьких группах, используя связанную за концы веревку, участники по команде ведущего должны создать форму определенной цифры, буквы, предмета.

小组合作，使用一个绳圈来塑造成数字、字母、形状或物体。

Küçük gruplar daire şeklinde bir halatla sayılar, harfler, şekiller ve objeler oluşturabilmek için beraber çalışırlar.

Grupos pequeños trabajan juntos para formar números, formas y objetos con una cuerda amarrada en círculo.

ロ「プを使い、「字や文字、ものの形など を表現します。

Цөөн хүний бүрээлдэхүүнтэй бүлгүүд хамтран олсон тойргийг ашиглан тоо, үсэг, дүрс, ямар нэгэн зүйл бүтээнэ.

Piccoli gruppi lavorano insieme per formare numeri, lettere, forme e oggetti usando un cerchio di corda.

Des petits groupes travaillent ensemble pour former des chiffres, lettres, formes et objets à partir d'une corde nouée en cercle.

קבוצות קטנות עובדות יחד ליצור מספרים, אותיות, צורות, וחפצים עם טבעת חבל.

Kleine groepjes werken samen om van een koord nummers, letters, vormen en voorwerpen te vormen.

Μικρές ομάδες συνεργάζονται για να σχηματίσουν αριθμούς, γράμματα, σχήματα και αντικείμενα με ένα σκοινί δεμένο σε κύκλο.

จับ กลุ่มเล็ก ๆทำงานด้ว ยกนั ช่วยกนั สร้า งรูปู ทรง ของตวั เลข ตวั อกั ษร และวตั ถุต่างๆดว้ ยเสน้ เชอื ก

Die Teilnehmer einer kleinen Gruppe bilden einen Kreis und sind durch ein Seil, dessen Enden miteinander verknotet sind, fest verbunden (Raccoon Circle). Nach Anweisung des Spielleiters bilden sie mit dem Seil Zahlen, Buchstaben, Formen und Gegenstände, ohne das Seil dabei loszulassen.

Små grupper arbejder sammen om at forme tal, bogstaver, former og ting, ved hjælp af et stykke reb.

Pequenos grupos trabalham juntos para formar números, letras, forma e objectos com um círculo de corda.

27 Three Chairs
Exploring Collaboration and Win/Win Behavior

This challenge provides an interesting debrief, since most groups tend to compete rather than searching for a win-win solution. The group is divided into three equal parts and each group is provided with one of the following commands:

1. Place all the chairs in a circle.

2. Turn all the chairs on their side.

3. Move all the chairs outside the room.

The group is instructed to carefully and quickly perform the task they are assigned. Chaos typically happens, leaving the opportunity for an inspired review of what happened, and a discussion about achieving a win-win solution when possible (such as placing all the chairs on their side, in a circle, outside the room).

English Russian Chinese Turkish Spanish Japanese Mongolian Italian

Three instructions, one given to each 1/3 of the group. 1. Place all chairs in a circle. 2. Turn all chairs on their side. 3. Take all chairs outside this room.

Делим участников на три равные группы. Каждая группа получает разные команды: 1. Поставить все стулья по кругу. 2. Поставить все стулья на бок. 3. Вынести все стулья из комнаты.

三项指令，每组获得一项指令完成任务。1. 把所有椅子围成一个圆圈。2. 将所有椅子放倒在地上。 3. 把所有椅子拿到房间外面。

Bir grubun 1/3'üne verilecek şekilde üç tane talimat: 1. Bütün sandalyeleri halka haline getirin. 2. Bütün sandalyeleri yanlarına doğru çevirin. 3. Bütün sandalyeleri odadan dışarı çıkarın.

Tres instrucciones, cada una se le dá a una tercera parte del grupo. 1. Pon todas las sillas en un círculo. 2.Acuesta todas las sillas de un lado. 3. Saca todas las sillas de este cuarto.

グル「プを3つに分け、それぞれに以下の指示を「えます。「1.すべての椅子を円形に配置する」「2.すべての椅子を「倒しにする」「3.すべての椅子を部屋の外に出す」

Оролцогчдод дараах гурван зааварчилгааг өгнө, нэгийг нь тухайн бүлгийн 1/3-т өгнө. 1. Сандлуудаа тойрог болгон тавина. 2. Бүх сандлуудаа хажуулдуулж тавина. 3. Бүх сандлуудаа энэ өрөөний гадна талд гаргана.

Tre istruzioni, ciascuna data ad un terzo del gruppo. 1. Mettere tutte le sedie in cerchio. 2. Ribaltare tutte le sedie 3. Portare tutte le sedie fuori da questa stanza.

Chaque tiers du groupe reçoit une consigne différente :1. Placer toutes les chaises en cercle. 2. Tourner toutes les chaises sur le côté. 3. Sortir toutes les chaises de la salle.

כל 1/3 קבוצה מקבל אחד משלוש הוראות: 1. שימו את כל הכיסאות במעגל. 2. השכיבו את כל הכיסאות על הצד. 3. הוציאו את כל הכיסאות מחוץ לחדר.

Verdeel de groep in drieën en geef elke groep een instructie: 1. Zet alle stoelen in een kring. 2. Zet alle stoelen op hun kant. 3. Zet alle stoelen uit de zaal.

Δίνονται τρείς οδηγίες, μία σε κάθε 1/3 της ομάδας. 1. Τοποθετήστε όλες τις καρέκλες σε κύκλο. 2. Γυρίστε όλες τις καρέκλες στο πλάι. 3. Βγάλτε όλες τις καρέκλες έξω από το δωμάτιο.

มีคำสั่งอยู่3คำสั่งโดยแบ่งไปให้แต่ละกลุ่มแบ่งย่อยเป็นก ลุ่มละ1ส่วน3ของจำนวนสมาชิกให้ได้   3กลุ่มคำสั่งแรกฏ ให้จัดเก้าอี้ให้เป็นรูปวงกลมคำสั่งสองให้ซ้อนเก้าอี้ขึ้นทางดา นข้างคำสั่งที่สามให้ยักเก้าอี้ออกไปจากห้อง

Eine Gruppe wird in 3 Teile aufgeteilt. Die Gruppenteile erhalten jeweils eine der folgenden Anweisungen, die sorgfältig und schnell auszuführen sind: 1. Stellt alle Stühle in einem Kreis auf. 2. Dreht alle Stühle auf der Stelle. 3. Tragt alle Stühle aus dem Raum.

Tre instruktioner bliver givet til en gruppe, som er delt i tre. Instruks til gruppe nr. 1: Anbring alle stole i en cirkel. Instruks til gruppe nr. 2: Lig alle stole ned på siden. Instruks til gruppe nr. 3: Tag alle stole ud af rummet.

Três instruções, uma é dada a cada 1/3 do grupo. 1. Disponha todas as cadeiras num círculo. 2. Vire as cadeiras de lado. 3. Leve as cadeiras para fora da sala.

116

28 Match Cards
A Character Building Activity

24 index cards are placed face down on each table. One group member at a time approaches the table and turns over any two cards. If these two cards match, they can remain face up in their original positions. If they do not match, they are turned face down and the next person approaches the table. The first team to turn over all 24 cards is the winner of that round. The value of this game is that the playing (word) cards become the debriefing tool, and a serious discussion can occur related to the content of the cards. For example, cards can include words describing character, such as: respect, trust, honesty, integrity, appreciating diversity, patience, teamwork, positive attitude, helpfulness, accountability, empathy and leadership.

When all cards have been turned over, invite each person to pick up a card that has a word they admire and discuss why they chose this card. Next, invite the group to discuss which five words are the most valued by the entire group.

The T&T Training Cards have 26 pairs of character words for this game. Or you can create your own collection by writing words that have meaning for your participants on 24 index cards.

The memory game with 24 cards. Turn over two cards, if they match, they remain face-up. If no match, they are turned face-down again. Discuss the words on the cards when all cards are face up.

Для игры нужны 24 карты, на каждой из которых написано какое-либо понятие. Переверните две карты. Если понятия подходят друг другу, оставьте карты перевернутыми. Если нет, поверните их вновь обложкой вверх. Обсудите все понятия, написанные на картах, когда закончите игру.

有24张卡片的记忆游戏。翻开两张卡片，如果卡片上的字匹配，可以将它们字面朝上放在桌上。如果不匹配则将卡片字面朝下放回原位。翻开所有卡片后和小组讨论卡片上的词。

24 kartlı bir hafıza oyunu. İki kart çevirin, eğer bu iki kart eşleşirlerse, masada yüzleri açık bir şekilde kalsınlar. Eşleşmezler ise kartları yüzükoyun bir şekilde tekrar eski haline çevirin. Bütün kartlar eşleştikten sonra kartlarda yazan kelimeler üzerine tartışın.

Juego de memoria de 24 tarjetas. Voltea dos tarjetas, si son iguales, se dejan boca arriba sobre la mesa. Si no coinciden se ponen boca abajo de nuevo. Conversen sobre las palabras en las tarjetas una vez que hayan logrado voltearlas todas.

24枚のカードを使った記憶ゲームです。2枚をめくって、同じカードが出たらその面を上にして置きます。もし違っていたら、元に戻します。すべてのカードが一致したら、カードに書かれた言葉について話し合います。

24 карттай ой тогтоолтын тоглоом. Хоёр картыг сөхөөд тэр хоёр таарч байвал ширээн дээр дээш нь харуулан орхино. Хэрвээ таарахгүй бол доош нь харуулан үлдээнэ. Бүх картуудыг сөхөж дээш харуулах үед картууд дээр бичигдсэн үгнүүдийн талаар ярилц.

Il gioco del Memory con 24 carte. Girate due carte, se corrispondono, rimangono girate faccia in su. Se non corrispondono, vengono girate di nuovo faccia in giù. Dopo che tutte le carte sono state girate e sono faccia in su, discutete le parole che sono riportate sulle carte.

Jeu de mémoire avec 24 cartes. Retournez deux cartes; si elles sont identiques, les garder face vers le haut sur la table. Si elles sont différentes, les remettre face vers le bas. Discuter à propos des mots sur les cartes une fois toutes les cartes retournées.

משחק זיכרון עם 24 קלפים. הפכו 2 קלפים: אם הם תואמים, הם נשארים חשופים, ואם לא תואמים, הופכים בחזרה. פתחו דיון על המילים שעל הקלפים כאשר כל הקלפים חשופים.

Memory spel met 24 kaarten. Draai twee kaarten om en als deze hetzelfde zijn, laat ze dan omgekeerd met de woorden zichtbaar op de tafel liggen. Zijn ze niet identiek, draai de kaarten dan weer om. Als alle kaarten zijn omgedraaid, bespreek dan de woorden die op de kaarten staan.

Παιχνίδι μνήμης με 24 κάρτες. Γυρίστε δύο κάρτες, αν ταιριάζουν παραμένουν ανοιχτές στο τραπέζι. Αν δεν ταιριάζουν, τις αναποδογυρίσετε ξανά. Συζητήστε τις λέξεις στις κάρτες όταν όλες οι κάρτες είναι γυρισμένες προς τα πάνω.

เกมส์ วามจา 24 การ์ด เปิดหงายการ์ด ขนี้ 2 ใบดวู' าตรงค่ำฎ นั หรือฮ ไม่ ฎ ง ตรงคู้ หห้ง งายไว่อั้ ยา งนนั้ ถา ไมต่รงค่ใหค้ว่าหน้าการ์ดกลบปไป่อ ยางเดมิช่วยกนนัพฺ๊ดูคุยความหมายของคาบนการ์ดทหีงายหน้าอยบู่่นโต๊ะ

Spielt ein Memory Spiel mit 24 Karten: Sobald zwei zusammen gehörende Karten aufgedeckt werden, bleiben sie aufgedeckt liegen. Alle Karten, die nicht zusammen gehören, werden wieder umgedreht. Sprecht über die Begriffe auf den Karten, wenn alle Karten aufgedeckt wurden.

Huskespil med 24 kort. Vend 2 kort af gangen. Hvis de danner et par forbliver de vendt opad. Hvis ikke vendes de om igen. Tal om kortenes ord, når alle par er fundet.

O jogo da memória contém 24 cartas. Vire duas cartas, conteúdo para cima, se as duas forem iguais ficam viradas para cima. Se as duas cartas não corresponderem, voltam se de novo para baixo. Discuta as palavras escritas nas cartas, quando todas elas estão viradas para cima.

119

29 Human Knot
A Classic Teambuilding Activity

Invite the members of your group to stand in a circle. Next, ask each person to reach across the circle and grasp right hands with another person and then grasp left hands with a different person. This configuration results in what can best be described as a human tangle or even a gordian knot.

The problem solving opportunity for this group is to un-knot themselves so they are again standing in a circle. The challenge is to do so without anyone in the group disconnecting their hands from their partners.

Depending upon the complexity of the knot formed, some groups may finish quickly while other groups need more time. For especially difficult knots, a visit from the 'Knot Doctor' is possible. The Knot Doctor allows one set of hands to be temporarily disconnected and then immediately re-connected in a different location, to facilitate a successful completion to this challenge.

In small groups, participants join hands in a tangle and then try to unknot the group and form one circle without disconnecting hands.

В небольших группах участники берут друг друга за руки, образуя спутанный клубок, а затем пытаются его развязать и образовать круг, не отпуская руки друг друга.

在小组中，参与者手拉手缠在一起，尝试在不松手的情况下解开这个结，围成一个圆圈。

Katılımcılar küçük gruplar halinde el ele tutuşarak bir düğüm oluştururlar ve sonra ellerini birbirinden ayırmadan bu düğümü bozup yeni bir halka oluşturmaya çalışırlar.

En grupos pequeños, los participantes se agarran de las manos de manera desordenada, buscando quedar enredados. Luego intentan desenredarse sin soltarse de las manos y quedar en un solo círculo.

小さなグル「プで適「に手をつなぎ合い、こんがらがった「態をつくります。手をつないだままで、ほぐしていき、輪になります。

Цөөн хүнтэй бүлгийн оролцогчид зангилаа үүсгэн гараа зөрүүлнэ, бүлгийн зангилааг тайлахыг хичээ, гараа салгалгүй нэг тойрог үүсгэнэ.

In piccoli gruppi, i partecipanti uniscono le mani in un groviglio e poi cercano di snodare il gruppo e formare un cerchio senza mai staccare le mani.

En petits groupes, les participants s'entremêlent les mains et essaient ensuite de démêler le nœud afin de former un cercle, sans se lâcher les mains. French

בקבוצות קטנות, המשתתפים מחברים ידיים בפלונטר, ואז מנסים להתיר את הפלונטר הקבוצתי וליצור מעגל אחד מבלי לנתק ידיים. Hebrew

In kleine groepen, deelnemers geven elkaar een hand zodat ze helemaal in de knoop zitten. Probeer dan als een groep uit de knoop te komen, zonder dat de handen worden losgelaten. Dutch

Σε μικρές ομάδες οι συμμετέχοντες ενώνουν χέρια στη μέση και τα μπερδεύουν. Μετά προσπαθούν να ξεμπερδευτούν και να σχηματίσουν έναν κύκλο χωρίς να αφήσουν τα χέρια τους. Greek

จบั กลุ่มกนั เลก็ ๆ ทุนคนจบั มอื กนั ใหแ้ ม่นแลว้ พยายาม คลายปมตดิ ขดั ของกลุ่มเพ่อื ตงั้ แถวใหเ ป็น วงกลมโดย ไมใ่หม้อืของแต่ละคนหลุดออกจากกนั Thai

8-10 Teilnehmer stehen eng zusammen und fassen sich jeweils ungeordnet mit zwei anderen Teilnehmern gegenüber an den Händen. Dann soll die Gruppe versuchen, den entstandenen Knoten zu lösen und einen Kreis zu bilden, ohne dabei die Hände loszulassen. German

I mindre grupper danner deltagerne en knude, ved at holde hinanden i hænderne på kryds og tværs. Løs knuden, som gruppen har dannet, uden der gives slip på hinandens hænder. Danish

Em pequenos grupos, os participantes dão as mãos entrelaçando-se. Depois disso, tentam desentrelaçar o grupo de forma a voltar ao circulo sem largar as mãos. Portuguese

30 Shoe Towers
Teambuilding With Simple Props

Here is an activity that combines creative problem solving and construction with very familiar props. Invite the members of your group to take off both shoes. Toss one shoe in one pile and the other shoe in another pile. Then divide the group into two teams.

Each of these teams takes one collection of shoes and attempts to create the tallest tower they can from only these resources.

English Groups attempt to build the tallest tower possible using just one shoe from each person.

Russian Командам нужно построить как можно более высокую башню, используя по одному ботинку каждого участника команды.

Chinese 小组成员每人贡献一只鞋，尝试搭建一座最高的塔。

Turkish Gruplar her bir katılımcının bir ayakkabısını kullanarak mümkün olan en yüksek kuleyi kurmaya çalışırlar.

Spanish Los grupos intentan formar la torre mas alta utilizando unicamente un zapato de cada uno.

Japanese グループのメンバーから片方ずつ靴を集め、できるだけ高く積み上げます。

Mongolian Оролцогчдын өрөөсөн гутлаар бүлгүүд хамгийн өндөр цамхаг босгоно.

Italian I gruppi cercano di costruire la torre più alta possibile usando soltanto una scarpa di ogni partecipante.

Les équipes tentent de bâtir la plus haute tour possible en utilisant seulement un soulier par participant.

קבוצות מנסות לבנות את המגדל הכי גבוה מנעל אחת של כל משתתף.

Groepen proberen om de hoogste toren mogelijk te bouwen met behulp van slechts één schoen van elke deelnemer.

οι ομάδες προσπαθούν να χτίσουν τον υψηλότερο δυνατόν πύργο χρησιμοποιώντας ένα παπούτσι από κάθε συμμετέχοντα.

แต่ละกลุ่มพยายูมสรา้ งหอคอยใหส้ ู ู ทสี่ ,ด โดย สรา งจากรองเทา ของเพอี นในกลุ่มคนละ 1 ขา ง

Die Teilnehmer werden auf zwei Gruppen aufgeteilt. Dann werfen sie jeweils einen ihrer Schuhe in die Mitte der zwei Gruppen und versuchen dann, aus den Schuhen den höchstmöglichen Turm zu bauen.

I gruppen skal deltagerne forsøge at bygge det højst mulige tårn, ved hjælp af en sko fra hver deltager.

Grupos, tentam construir uma torre o mais alto possível utilizando apenas um sapato de cada participante.

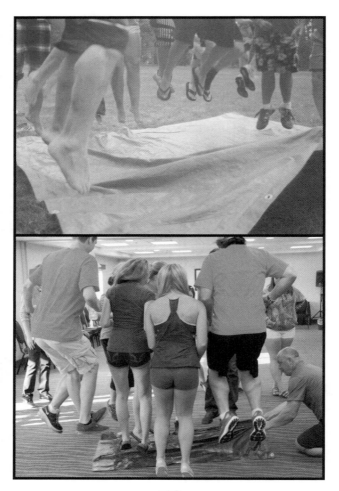

31 Team Tarp Jump
Teambuilding With Split Second Timing

Here is a team challenge that requires communication, teamwork and timing. Begin by inviting twelve or more people to stand on a plastic tarp. Next, ask for one volunteer to be the 'puller.'

The challenge is for the entire team to jump straight up and for the puller to pull the tarp completely out from under the team while they are in the air, so that they all land on the ground.

While standing on a tarp, challenge ten or more people to jump straight up and then pull the tarp out from underneath them before they touch the ground again.

10 и более участников стоят на брезенте, один рядом. Его задача успеть выдернуть брезент из-под членов своей команды, когда они дружно подпрыгнут вверх.

让10人或更多人站在一块油布上，挑战能否让所有人垂直跳起来后落地前将油布拉出来。

Bir muşambanın üstünde duran on ya da daha fazla kişi aynı anda zıplamaya çalışır ve daha sonra başka bir kişi ise onların ayakları tekrardan yere değmeden altlarındaki muşambayı düzgün bir şekilde ayaklarının altından çeker.

Mientras estan parados sobre una lona, reta al grupo a intentar saltar todos al mismo tiempo de manera que permitan que una persona retire la lona antes de que todos aterricen.

10人以上でタ┌プの上でジャンプし、着地する前にタ┌プを引き┌きます。

Берзентэн дээр зогсох зуураа арав юмуу түүнээс олон хүнийг эгц дээшээ үсрэхийг уриална. Дараа нь үсэрсэн хүмүүсийг газарт буухаас өмнө берзентийг тэдний дорооос амжилттай суга татан авах ёстой.

Dieci o più persone stanno in piedi su un telo. Tutti insieme saltano verso l'alto e, prima che atterrino di nuovo, bisogna riuscire a sfilare il telo da sotto.

Debout sur une toile, lancez le défi à dix personnes ou plus de sauter droit dans les airs puis de retirer la toile de sous leur pieds avant qu'ils ne retouchent le sol.

בזמן שעומדים על משטח, נאתגר עשרה אנשים או יותר לקפוץ ישר למעלה, ולמשוך החוצה את המשטח מתחתם לפני שהם נוחתים על הרצפה.

Tien of meer personen staan op een zeildoek. Daag ze uit door allemaal op te springen zodat het zeildoek onder ze uit getrokken kan worden, voordat de groep weer op de grond belandt.

Καθώς στέκονται σε έναν μουσαμά, προκαλέστε δέκα ή παραπάνω παίκτες να πηδήξουν ψηλά και μετά αποπειραθείτε να τραβήξετε το μουσαμά από κάτω τους πριν ακουμπήσουν ξανά στο έδαφος.

ในระหว่างทยี นี อยบู่ นผนี พลาสตกิ ใหช้ วนเพื่อ นฺๆอกี 10 คน หรอี มากกว่ามายนี บนผนี พลาสตกิ แลว้ ใหทุ้กคนกระโดดขนึท่า ตรงในอากาศโดยให้ใคนในกลุ่มทาหน้าทดีงีผนีพลาสตกิออกจากพนี ในระหว่างททีุกคนกระโดด ขนึเพื่อใหทุ้กคนลงมายนีบนพนืใดส้าเรจ็

Zehn oder mehr Teilnehmer stehen auf einer Plane, während eine Person außerhalb der Plane steht. Die Aufgabe des Außenstehenden ist es, die Teilnehmer der Gruppe dazu zu bringen, gleichzeitig in die Höhe zu springen, so dass er die Plane unter ihnen heraus ziehen kann, bevor sie wieder den Boden berühren.

Mens deltagerne står på en presenning, udfordres de til at hoppe lige op i luften, mens presenningen rives væk under dem, inden de rammer jorden/gulvet igen.

Enquanto em pé numa lona, desafie 10 ou mais pessoas a saltar para cima em simultâneo, e com sucesso puxe a lona por de baixo deles, antes que toquem no chão.

32 Community Juggling
A Teambuilding Challenge

Begin with a circle of ten people. A single tennis ball is used to establish a pattern of ball tossing within the group (the goal is to have the ball touch each person in the group just once before returning to the first thrower). Once established, this pattern remains throughout the activity. After the initial pattern is established, the game progresses by adding more balls (or soft throwable items, such as stuffed animals, toys, etc.) Five objects is a suitable goal for groups of 10 people. For variation, the pattern can be reversed (thrown in the opposite direction).

In a small group, establish a pattern and toss a ball to each member of the group. Next, add more balls, using the same pattern. Then reverse the direction.

В небольшой группе придумайте схему движения мяча так, чтобы он доходил до каждого участника игры. Затем увеличьте количество мячей. Наконец, запустите мячи в противоположном направлении.

在一个小组中，建立一个规则，向每个组员投递一个网球。接下来，使用同一个规则，加入更多的球。之后，逆向投掷。

Küçük gruplar halinde bir sıra belirleyip, tenis topunu her bir elemana sıraya uygun olarak atın. Devamında, aynı sırayı uygulayarak daha fazla top ekleyin. Daha sonra yönü tam tersine çevirip devam edin.

En un grupo pequeño, intenten lanzar una pelota de tenis a cada uno de los participantes, siguiendo un mismo orden (sin pasarlo a las personas que tienen al lado). Una vez logrado agrega mas pelotas de tenis y siguen usando el mismo orden de lanzamiento. Tambien puedes revertir ese orden.

グループで輪になり、順番を決めながら全員が「れるように、テニスボ「ルをパスします。次にボ「ルを追加して、複「のボ「ルが順番どおりにパスされるようにします。うまくいったら、逆方向にパスします。

Цөөн хүнтэй бүлгийн гишүүд ямар нэгэн хэлбэр гаргаад бүлгийн гишүүн бүр луу чиглүүлэн теннисийн бөмбөг шиднэ. Дараа нь энэ хэлбэрээр илүү олон бөмбөг нэмээд эсрэг чигт шиднэ.

In un piccolo gruppo, stabilire una sequenza e passarsi una pallina da tennis secondo la sequenza determinata. Successivamente aggiungere più palline mantenendo la stessa sequenza. Ripetere poi invertendo la direzione dei passaggi.

En petits groupes, établissez un circuit et lancer une balle de tennis à chaque membre du groupe. Ensuite, ajouter des balles, en suivant le même circuit. Puis, changer de direction.

בקבוצה קטנה, קבעו רצף וזרקו כדור טניס לכל משתתף בקבוצה. אח"כ הוסיפו עוד כדורים באותו הרצף. בסוף, הפכו את הכיוון.

In een kleine groep, stel een patroon vast en gooi een tennisbal naar iedere persoon in de groep. Vervolgens, voeg meer ballen toe die in hetzelfde patroon gegooid moeten worden. Wijzig daarna de richting en gooi in tegenovergestelde richting.

Σε μια μικρή ομάδα κάντε μια σειρά κινήσεων πετώντας μια μπάλα του τένις σε κάθε μέλος της ομάδας.

จับ กลุ่มเล็ก ๆ คิด ท่าทางวิธี กี่ารโยนลูกู เทนนิสไปให้ พ่อ นในกลุ่มแต่ละคน ต่อไปใหม พมิ จานวนลูกู เทนนิสแลว้โยน ตามวธิีที่คิดไว้แลว้ลองโยนยอ้นกลบัมา

Überlegt Euch in einer kleinen Gruppe ein Muster, nach dem Ihr Euch einen Tennisball zuwerft. Dabei muss der Ball von jedem Teilnehmer einmal berührt werden, bevor er auf den Teilnehmer trifft, der den Anfang gemacht hat. Nach kurzem Einüben des Musters werden weitere Bälle in die Gruppe hinein geworfen, die mit dem gleichen Muster zugeworfen werden. Dann Richtungswechsel.

I små grupper etableres et kaste mønster, hvor en tennisbold kaste rundt mellem gruppen medlemmer. Derefter sættes flere bolde i gang, men i det samme mønster. Derefter vendes retningen.

Num pequeno grupo, estabeleça um padrão e atire uma bola de ténis a cada membro do grupo. De seguida, acrescente mais bolas ao jogo, utilizando o mesmo padrão. Depois troque o sentido.

135

136

33 A Perfect Match
A Communication Challenge

Each member of a blindfolded group is presented with a single object. The challenge is for the group to discuss and identify which two objects in the group are identical twins of each other, while blindfolded (or eyes closed).

For this activity, it is helpful to choose a collection of objects which are somewhat similar and yet easy to identify (even with your eyes closed) such as: toys, beads, wood blocks, keys, nuts & bolts, coins or plastic bottle caps.

English

With their eyes closed, groups discuss the objects they are holding and attempt to identify two objects that are identical from their total collection.

Russian

Группе игроков завязывают глаза и выдают некие предметы, два из которых идентичны друг другу. Задача команды обсудить свою коллекцию предметов и выявить идентичные.

Chinese

小组成员闭着眼睛来讨论他们手中的物品，尝试从所有物品中找出两个完全相同的物品。

Turkish

Gruplar gözleri kapalı bir halde ellerinde tuttukları nesneler üzerine tartışıp, tamamıyla aynı olan iki nesneyi bulmaya çalışırlar.

Spanish

Con los ojos cerrados el grupo conversa sobre objetos que tienen en sus manos e intentan identificar los 2 objetos que son exactamente iguales.

Japanese

目「しをしたメンバ「同士で各「が手に持っているものについて「明し、同じもの同士のペアをつくります。

Mongolian

Бүлгүүд нүдээ аниастайгаар барьсан зүйлийнхээ талаар ярилцаж нийт цуглуулгаас хоёр зүйлийг тодорхойлохыг оролдох хэрэгтэй.

Italian

Ad occhi chiusi il gruppo discute degli oggetti che ciascuno ha in mano e cerca di identificare, tra tutti gli oggetti presenti, i due oggetti identici tra loro.

Avec les yeux fermés, les groupes discutent des objets dont ils disposent et tentent d'identifier deux objets identiques parmi l'ensemble de leur collection.

בעיניים עצומות, קבוצות מדברות על החפצים שהם מחזיקים ומנסים לזהות שני חפצים זהים מתוך כל האוסף.

Met de ogen dicht discussieert de groep over het voorwerp wat iedereen vast heeft. Op deze manier proberen ze twee identieke exemplaren te vinden uit alle voorwerpen die binnen de groep aanwezig zijn.

Με τα μάτια κλειστά οι ομάδες συζητούν για τα αντικείμενα που κρατούν και προσπαθούν να εντοπίσουν δύο ίδια αντικείμενα από την πλήρη συλλογή.

สมาชกิ ทุกคนจะถูกปิดตาไว้ พ่อี ใหพ้ ดู คุยกนั เกยี วกบั สงิ ของทไี่ ขาถอี อยู่ว่ามนั มรี ปู ทรงอย่างไร เพ่อี ช่วยกนัต อบว่าวตัถุ2ชนิ้นัน้เปน็แบบเดยีวกนัหรอไีม่

Die Teilnehmer tauschen sich mit geschlossenen Augen über Gegenstände aus, die sie in Händen halten. Sie versuchen heraus zu bekommen, welche zwei Gegenstände identisch sind.

Med lukkede øjnen diskuterer gruppen de ting de holder og forsøger at identificere to ting, der er identiske fra deres samlede kollektion af ting.

Com os olhos fechados, os grupos discutem os objectos que estão a segurar e tentam identificar dois objectos idênticos do total da sua colecção.

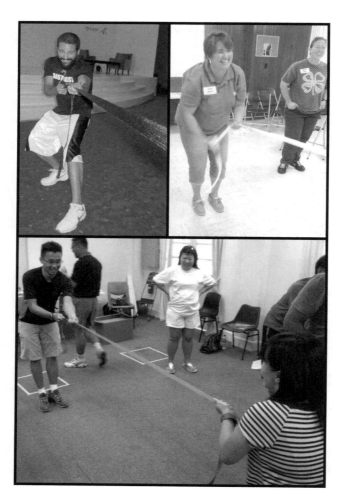

34 Rope Jousting
A Physical Contest

This physical challenge begins with two people holding opposite ends of a rope 15 feet (5 meters) long. If one person can make their opponent take a step in any direction or let go of the rope, they win! In this game, strategy is as important as strength and balance.

If you wish to increase the level of challenge for this activity, invite each player to stand with their feet together (right and left foot touching each other - as shown by the player in the photograph on this page).

English Two people attempt to unbalance their partner using a piece of rope.

Russian Двое игроков стараются перетянуть на себя канат.

Chinese 两个人拉一条绳子，尝试让对方失去平衡。

Turkish İki kişi halatı çekerek karşı taraftakinin dengesini bozmaya çalışır.

Spanish Dos personas intentan de hacer perder el balance de su pareja utilizando un pedazo de cuerda.

Japanese 2人がロープの端を持って、相手がバランスを崩すようかけ引きをします。

Mongolian Хоёр хүн олс ашиглан нэг нэгнийхээ тэнцвэрийг алдагдуулахыг оролдоно.

Italian Usando uno spezzone di corda cercare di far perdere l'equilibrio al proprio partner.

142

Deux personnes tentent de faire perdre l'équilibre à leur partenaire en utilisant un bout de corde.

שני אנשים מנסים לגרום אחד לשני לאבד את שיווי המשקל ע"י שימוש בחתיכת חבל.

Twee personen proberen elkaar uit balans te brengen met een stuk touw.

Δύο παίκτες προσπαθούν να βγάλουν τον συμπαίκτη τους εκτός ισορροπίας, χρησιμοποιώντας ένα κομμάτι σκοινί.

แข่งขันักนัสองคนโดยพยายามทาให้เพ่อืนอกีฝ่ายหนึ่งเสยีการทรงตวัโดยการกระตุกหรอืเหวยีง ปลายเชอื ก

Zwei Teilnehmer halten ein Seil jeweils an einem Ende und versuchen, ihr Gegenüber aus der Balance zu bringen.

To deltagere skal forsøge af få modparten ud af balance, med et reb de holder imellem hinanden.

Duas pessoas tentam desequilibrar o seu parceiro, utilizando um bocado de corda.

Wah!

35 Wah!
My Favorite Game - Just For Fun!

Wah is a game of the samurai (well, probably not, but it is fun to frame it that way!) So when you say, 'Wah!' you need to say it like a samurai, 'WAH!' There are three basic movments to this game.

Begin with multiple circles of about 8 people in Wah ready position - feet slightly spread (like the capital letter A), hands together. In each circle, one person volunteers to begin the game. This first person makes eye contact with another person, points to them with both hands and says, "Wah!" The second person now raises both of their hands straight up over their head and says, "Wah!" The third and final move involves the two people standing on each side of person two, who make non-contact lumberjack chopping motions towards person number two, and also say "Wah!" If each person completes their task and says 'Wah!' with gusto and on time, the game continues. But, if anyone is early or late in the performance of their duty, or they make a mistake, they are 'out' of the game. But the good news is, they are not permanently out of the game. They can quickly move to another circle and immediately get back into the game.

After the third movement is completed, person number two (whose hands are still raised high above their head) becomes the first person in the next round, points to one of their group members and evokes the command, "Wah!" And the game continues.

Circles of people pass the Wah! around the group. Anyone making a mistake moves to a different circle and continues to play.

Игроки по определенной схеме «передают» в кругу «Вау». Тот, кто ошибся, выходит из своего круга и продолжает играть в другом.

大家围成一圈传递哇！每个出错的人都可以换到一个新的圈子里继续游戏。

Halka halindeki elemanlar grubun içinde "Wah" sözünü yayarlar. Hata yapan başka bir halkaya geçer ve oyuna devam eder.

En círculos, las personas van pasando el Wah! Cuando una persona se equivoca sale de ese círculo y sigue jugando en otro.

輪になって、決められた手順で動作をしながら「ワ「！」と言います。動きとタイミングを間違えた場合は、その輪を離れ、別の輪に入ってゲ「ムを「けます。

Бүлгээрээ Ура! гэж чангаар хэлэн тойрч зогссон хүмүүст дамжуулна. Алдаа гаргасан хүн өөр тойрог руу шилжин үргэлжлүүлэн тоглоно.

In cerchio le persone si passano il Wah! Chi commette uno sbaglio va in un altro cerchio e continua a giocare.

Des personnes en cercle passent le Wah! autour du groupe. Si quelqu'un se trompe, il change de cercle et continue à jouer.

מעגלים של אנשים מעבירים את ה"ווה" (Wah!) סביב הקבוצה. מי שטועה, עובר למעגל אחר וממשיך לשחק.

In een kring geven deelnemers de "Wah!" door aan de groep. Als iemand een fout maakt, gaat deze persoon door naar een andere kring en speelt daar door.

Σε κύκλο οι παίκτες λένε Wa!, ο ένας μετά τον άλλο. Όποιος κάνει λάθος μεταφέρεται σε διαφορετικό κύκλο και συνεχίζει να παίζει.

ตั้ง วงกลมเป็นวงกว้า งแลว้ ส่งต่อ ว้า! ไปรอบๆวง ใครทาผดิ จง้ หวะจะตอ้ งเรมิ ตน้ ว้า! ใหมไ ปเรอี ยๆ

Die Teilnehmer spielen die Wah!-Choreografie innerhalb der Gruppe durch. Wenn einer einen Fehler macht, verlässt er den Kreis und wechselt in einen der anderen Wah!-Kreise und macht dort mit.

I forskellige cirkler giver deltagerne "wah" videre i gruppen. Den, der laver en fejl, går over i en anden gruppe og spiller videre.

Círculos de pessoas passam o "Wah!" em volta do grupo. Alguém que faça um erro troca de circulo e continua a jogar.

147

36 Pulse
A Table Game for Groups

Begin with a group of players seated, with one hand flat on a table. The group leader begins the pulse by pointing in the direction the pulse will begin to travel (left or right) and then tapping the table once with their hand. The pulse moves in the direction stated and the next person continues by tapping the table once as the pulse continues to travel around the table. At any point, a player can tap the table once or twice. If they tap once, the pulse continues in the same direction. If they tap twice, the pulse reverses direction. If anyone around the table lifts even a single finger when it is not their turn, they lose that hand for the duration of the round. Play continues in each round until approximately half of the group has been eliminated.

Round One - players place just one hand on the table.
Round Two - players use both hands, side-by-side.
Round Three - players use both hands, but cross them (to form an X) so that their right hand crosses over the left.
Round Four - players use both hands, but reach outwards so that their right hand crosses over the left hand of the person on their right and their left hand crosses over the right hand of the person on their left.
Round Five - players place their hands side-by-side and an additional movement is allowed. If a player thumps the table with a fist, the pulse jumps over the next hand in that direction. If they make a fist and double-thump the table, the pulse reverses direction and skips a hand in that direction.

A table game where hands are used to pass a pulse (hand slap) around the table. First with one hand, then two hands and finally with hands crossed.

Игра за столом, в которой хлопком по кругу передается «пульс» группы. Сначала играют одной рукой, затем двумя и, наконец, двумя пересеченными руками.

通过用手拍击桌面来传递节拍的桌面游戏。开始时使用一只手，然后双手，最后双手交叉。

Bu ellerin masanın üzerine vurulmasıyla (masaya bir tokat indirmekle) oynanan bir masa oyunu. Önce bir el, sonra iki el ve sonuçta bütün eller birbirine girecek şekilde oynanır.

Un juego de mesa en el que se usan las manos para pasar un impulso (manotón) por la mesa. Primero con una mano, luego con dos y al final con las manos cruzadas.

机を手で叩くことでパルスを送るテ「ブルゲ「ムです。最初は片手で、次は「手で、最後は隣の人と手を交差させて行います。

Ширээ тойрон зогсоод гараараа хэмнэлтэй цохилт хийж түүнийг дамжуулан тоглодог ширээний тоглоом. Эхлээд нэг гараараа, дараа нь хоёр гараараа сүүлд нь гараа зөрүүлэн ширээгээ цохино.

Si gioca intorno ad un tavolo. Le mani si usano per passare un impulso (schiaffo) intorno al tavolo. Prima una mano, poi due mani e da ultimo con le mani incrociate.

Un jeu de table dans lequel les mains sont utilisées pour faire passer le pouls (tape dans la main) autour de la table. D'abord avec une main, puis avec deux mains et finalement avec les mains croisées.

משחק שולחן שבו משתמשים בידיים כדי להעביר פעימה (מכה ביד על השולחן) סביב השולחן. קודם עם יד אחת, אח"כ עם שתי ידיים, ולבסוף עם ידיים שלובות.

Een tafelspel waarbij je door middel van je handen op de tafel te klappen een ritme doorgeeft rondom de tafel. Eerst met één hand dan twee handen en tot slot met gekruiste handen.

Ένα επιτραπέζιο παιχνίδι, όπου τα χέρια χρησιμοποιούνται για να περάσουν ένα σφυγμό (χτυπάμε με την παλάμη του δεξιού μας χεριού την παλάμη του δεξιού χεριού του παίκτη που βρίσκεται αριστερά μας) σε όλον τον κύκλο. Πρώτα με το ένα χέρι, μετά με τα δύο και μετά με τα χέρια σταυρωμένα.

เล่นเกมสบ์ นโต๊ะ โดยใช้มือ อี เป็นตัว้ สร้้ งจงั หวะตลี งบุน โต๊ะไปรอบๆ เริ่ จากมือ หนึ่งขา ง และเพิ่มิ เป็น สองขาง จนใช้มือีไขวก้นักากาหนดจงหวะตี

Ein Tischspiel, bei dem mit den Händen ein Impuls (durch einen Schlag auf den Tisch) im Kreis um den Tisch herum weiter gegeben wird. Zuerst spielt jeder nur mit einer Hand mit, dann mit beiden und schließlich mit überkreuzten Armen.

En leg hvor hænderne bliver brugt til at give en puls (hånd klap) videre rundt om bordet. Først med 1 hånd, derefter med 2 hænder og til sidst med krydsede hænder.

Um jogo de mesa onde as mãos são utilizadas para passar uma pulsação (uma pequena 'chapadinha' na mão) em volta da mesa. Primeiro com uma mão, depois com duas e finalmente de mãos cruzadas.

Nose Jousting

37 Nose Jousting
A Unique Competition

This playfully competitive game requires a roll of masking tape and lots of people. First, provide a 4 inch (100mm) long piece of masking tape to every participant. Invite them to roll the tape into a loop (sticky side out) and stick this masking tape loop to their nose. When two players meet, they touch noses together and then pull back. One of the two people will capture (win) both pieces of tape. The loser is not out of the game, they become the cheering section by standing behind the winner, hands on the winner's shoulders and chanting the winner's name as they continue their quest to become the 'intergalactic nose jousting champion.'

Winners should play other winners with approximately the same number of people in their cheering sections.

With each respective round, the number of people following their champion increases, until just two long lines remain. In this final round, the sound volume is incredible as the two remaining champions face off, press their noses together, and one champion is victorious!

With masking tape on their noses, players touch noses and pull back. The player keeping the tape is the winner. Play continues until one champion is found.

Игроки закрепляют на носу кусочек двустороннего скотча и касаются носами друг друга. Выигрывает тот, на чьем носу остался скотч. Игра продолжается до определения единственного победителя.

用胶带粘在鼻子上，队员碰鼻子然后向后拉。鼻子上留有胶带的队员胜利，并继续游戏直到最后一个人胜出游戏。

Oyuncular burunlarındaki maske bandıyla diğer oyuncunun burnuna dokunup onun maskesini çekip bırakırlar. Maske bantı düşmemiş olan oyuncu galip olur ve yeni bir galip bulunana kadar oyun devam eder.

Cada participante tiene un pedazo de tirro pegado en su nariz, los jugadores chocan nariz con nariz. El jugador que se queda con el tirro del otro es el ganador y continua jugando hasta que uno de ellos se queda con todos los tirros y es el Campeón.

マスキングテープで粘着面が外になった輪をつくり、鼻に貼ります。相手とテープ同士をひっつけてから離し、テープが鼻に乗った方が勝ちです。優勝者が決まるまでゲームを続けます。

Цаасан туузыг хамар дээр наагаад тоглогчид нэг нэгийхээ хамарт хүрч туузыг унагаана. Туузыг тогтоож чадсан нь ялагч болж, хамгийн сүүлчийн аварга шалгарах хүртэл тоглоно.

Con del nastro adesivo di carta sul naso, i giocatori si toccano naso contro naso. Quando si staccano, il giocatore che mantiene il nastro adesivo sul proprio naso vince. Il gioco continua fino a quando non si trova il campione assoluto.

Avec du ruban adhésif sur le nez, les joueurs se touchent le nez et se retirent. Le joueur qui conserve le morceau de ruban est vainqueur et le jeu se poursuit jusqu'à ce qu'il y ait un grand champion.

שמים נייר דבק (מסקינג טייפ) על האף. השחקנים נוגעים אף באף ומושכים לאחור. השחקן ששומר את נייר הדבק הוא המנצח, וממשיכים לשחק עד שיש אלוף אחד.

Met afplakband aan hun neus, spelers raken elkaars neuzen aan en trekken dan terug. De speler die het afplakband aan zijn neus houdt, is de winnaar en speelt door totdat één ultieme kampioen gevonden is.

Με χαρτοταινία στις μύτες τους, οι παίκτες ακουμπούν τις μύτες τους και απομακρύνονται. Ο παίκτης που συνεχίζει να έχει την χαρτοταινία στη μύτη του είναι ο νικητής και συνεχίζει να παίζει, μέχρι να μείνει μόνο ένας.

ให้ ปะเทปกาวไวท้ จี มกู แลว้ ผู้ ล่น 2 คนเอาจมกู มาชนกนั เพ่อื ใชจ้ มกู ของเรวดงึ เทปก้าวจากจมกู ของ อกี คนหน่งึ ออกมา,กจ์ ะเป็นผชู้ นะ แขง่ ขนั ต่อไปเร่อื ยๆจนกว่าจะได้ผ์ ชู้ นะคนสุดทา ย

Mit Malerkrepp an der Nase, berühren sich zwei Teilnehmer an der Nase und ziehen den Kopf zurück. Der Teilnehmer, der dem anderen das Klebeband abgejagt hat, ist der Gewinner und spielt weiter, bis der ultimative Nasenklebeband-Champion als einziger übrig ist.

Med tape på næsen rører deltagerne hinandens næser og hiver baglæns. Den deltager, hvis tape forbliver på næsen, har vundet. Legen fortsætter til den ultimative vinder er fundet.

Com fita adesiva de dupla face no nariz, os jogadores tocam narizes e puxam para trás. O jogador que mantém a fita adesiva no nariz é o vencedor e continua a jogar, até haver um campeão.

38 Pirate's Treasure
A Communication Competition

This communication activity requires two teams of four people. Team One has a blindfolded *Seeker* that is on their hands and knees trying to find an object in the grass. There are also two *Lookers* who can see the *Seeker* but cannot speak, and one *Communicator* who can speak and who can see the Lookers but has their back to the Seeker so they cannot see them. Team Two has a blindfolded *Whomper* who wields a long foam pool noodle and tries to contact (Whomp!) the Seeker. There are also two *Lookers* and one *Communicator* in Team Two.

Each team is trying to be the first to complete their task. The Seeker is trying to find an object in the grass, such as a tennis ball, stuffed animal or even a cowbell. The Whomper is trying to contact the Seeker with their foam noodle. The Lookers are giving hand motion instructions to the Communicator who is shouting directions to the Seeker (or Whomper). First team to accomplish their task twice, wins! Then have team members change roles and play again.

Two teams of 4 people work together to communicate the location of an object. The Seeker tries to find the object. The Whomper tries to whomp the seeker.

2 команды по 4 человека в каждой коммуницируют друг с другом, чтобы определить местонахождение некого объекта. Охотник старается найти предмет, а Чудовище старается настичь охотника.

2个4人小组合作来沟通一件物品的位置。搜寻者尽力去找到该物品。撞击者设法击中搜寻者。

Dört kişilik takımlar nesnenin yerini bulabilmek için birlikte çalışırlar. Nesneyi arayın objeyi bulmaya çalışırken, ebe ise arayanı yenmeye/ebelemeye çalışır.

Dos equipos de 4 personas trabajan juntos para comunicar la ubicación de un objeto. El que busca, intenta de encontrar el objeto. El WHOMPER intenta de Whompear el que busca.

4人組の2チ「ムで「「する、「探しゲ「ムです。「索係 (Seeker) は「物を探し、攻「係 (Whomper) は「索係を攻「します。

Дөрвөн хүний бүрэлдэхүүнтэй хоёр баг хамтарч нэг обьектийн байршлын талаар харилцан ярилцана. Хайгч тухайн обьектийг олохыг эрмэлзэнэ. Үймүүлэгч хайгчид саад болохыг оролдоно.

Due gruppi di quattro persone cercano di comunicare la collocazione di un oggetto. Il Cercatore tenta di trovare l'oggetto. Il Battitore cerca di colpire il Cercatore.

Deux équipes de quatre personnes travaillent ensemble afin de communiquer où se situe un objet. Le chercheur essaie de trouver l'objet. Le Chasseur essaie de toucher le chercheur.

שתי קבוצות של ארבעה אנשים עובדים יחד לתקשר ביניהם מיקום של חפץ. המחפש (Seeker) מנסה למצוא את החפץ. המרביץ (Whomper) מנסה להכות את המחפש.

Twee groepen van vier personen werken samen door goed te communiceren waar de locatie van het voorwerp zich bevindt. De zoeker (Seeker) probeert het voorwerp te vinden. De beuker (Whomper) probeert de zoeker door middel van een schuimrubberen honkbalknuppel de zoeker uit te schakelen.

Δύο ομάδες των τεσσάρων ατόμων συνεργάζονται για να επικοινωνήσουν την τοποθεσία ενός αντικειμένου. Ένας παίκτης προσπαθεί να βρει το αντικείμενο και ένας άλλος προσπαθεί να τον πετύχει με ένα μακαρόνι πισίνας.

จบั กลุ่ม 4 คนมา 2 กลุ่ม เพื่อ ช่วยกนั บอกเพื่อ นว่าสิ่ ของวางอยู่ตู รงไหน เพื่อ นทที่ หน้าที่ เป็น "ผู้ คน้หา"พยายามฟังคาสงัแลว้หาของ ใหเจอโดยเรว่ ส่วนอกีทมีหนงึ่จะส่งคนออกมาสกดัผคู้น้หาของทมีเรา

Zwei Teams aus je 4 Leuten arbeiten gegeneinander. Das „Seeker-Team" versucht, allein mittels Kommunikation, den blinden Seeker zu einem Gegenstand im Spielfeld zu führen. Das „Whomper-Team" versucht, seinen Whomper so zu lenken, dass er dies verhindern kann, indem er dem Seeker mit seiner Schwimmnudel trifft.

To hold, med hver fire deltagere, samarbejder om at finde et objekt. "søgeren" prøver at finde objektet. "Whompen" prøver at "wumpe" den der søger.

Duas equipas de quatro pessoas trabalham em equipa para comunicar a localização de um objecto. O "Seeker" tenta encontrar o objecto. O "Whomper" tenta "bater" no "Seeker"

39 BUMP
A (Very) Physical Energizer

In this game, small groups of people stand inside a knotted Raccoon Circle (rope circle) on the ground. These people face outward and place their hands on their knees. The challenge is to bump all of the other people out of the circle. Last person in the circle, wins!

Because this is a very physical game, be sure to use this activity only when you have a safe, open space. Once any part of your body (such as your foot) touches the ground outside the rope circle, you are eliminated from the game.

English Russian Chinese Turkish Spanish Japanese Mongolian Italian

Small groups inside a circle bump into each other (backwards) until 1 person remains inside the circle.

Небольшие группы игроков стоят внутри круга, спиной к центру круга, руки на коленках. Круг обозначен канатом. Игроки толкают друг друга за пределы круга, пока в кругу не останется один единственный победитель.

小组队员在一个绳圈中用背部撞击彼此出圈，直到绳圈中仅剩一人。

Halka halindeki halatın içindeki küçük gruplar halkanın içerisinde tek bir kişi kalıncaya kadar birbirlerine (arkadan) çarparlar.

En grupos pequeños, parados dentro de una cuerda amarrada en circulo, los participantes caminan en retroceso, chocando de espaldas con el resto de los participantes, intentando sacarlos del area, hasta que queda una sola persona.

ロｰプでつくった輪の中にｰ人が背中合わせで立ち、ぶつかり合ってほかの人を追い出します。最後までｰった人が勝者です。

Олсон тойргийн дотор цөөн хүнтэй бүлгээр орж нэг нэгийгээ нуруугаар нь түлхэж тоглоно, тойрог дотор үлдэж чадсан нэг хүн ялагч болно.

In piccoli gruppi, dentro un cerchio di corda, ci si scontra l'uno contro l'altro (all'indietro) fino a quando ua sola persona rimane nel cerchio.

Des petits groupes à l'intérieur d'un cercle de corde se foncent dedans (à reculons) jusqu'à ce qu'il ne reste qu'une seule personne dans le cercle.

קבוצות קטנות בתוך מעגל חבל מתנגשים אחד בשני (הפוך) עד שנשאר רק אדם אחד בפנים.

Kleine groepen binnen een cirkel van touw botsen ruggelings tegen elkaar. Degene die als laatste overblijft in de cirkel, heeft gewonnen.

Μικρές ομάδες μέσα σε έναν κύκλο από σκοινί συγκρούονται πλάτη με πλάτη, μέχρι να παραμείνει μόνο ένας μέσα στον κύκλο.

จับ กลุ่มเล็ก ๆ เข้า ไปอยู่ ในวงกลมของเชือ ก หนั หลัง ชนกน แลว้ พยายามบมี้ เพื่อ นให้ห้ ลุดออกไป นอก วงจนเหลอีคนเดยีวในวงจงึเป็นผชู้นะ

Stellt Euch in einen Kreis innerhalb eines Seils, mit dem Rücken zum Kreisinneren und leicht gebeugt mit den Händen an den Knien. Versucht dann, die anderen Teilnehmer aus dem Seilkreis heraus zu drängen. Sieger ist, wer als letzter Teilnehmer noch im Kreis steht.

En lille gruppe, inde i en cirkel, som er formet af reb, skal forsøge at skubbe hinanden ud af cirkelen (der skubbes kun med ryggen/bagdelen) indtil kun en person er tilbage, inde i cirklen.

Pequenos grupos dentro de um circulo de corda dão encontrões uns nos outros (de costas) até que apenas uma pessoa fique dentro do circulo.

163

40 The Dice Game
A Table Game Just For Fun

Here is my favorite dice game. Simple too! You'll need two dice, one index card for each player and a single pen for this game. To begin, one person in the group rolls the dice. If they happen to get doubles, the group members yell, "doubles," and that person takes the pen and begins writing on their card the numbers, 1, 2, 3, 4,... Meanwhile, the dice continue to be passed around the circle. When another player rolls doubles, the group members again yell, "doubles," and that person gets the pen and begins writing. The first person to write from one to one hundred on their index card, wins!

For variety, once a player writes to the number 50, they must change hands and write with their non-dominant hand for numbers 51 to 100.

Players that roll doubles grab the pen and write on their card the numbers from 1 to 100. First person to reach 100 wins!

Игрок, которому удалось выбросить дубль на кубиках, берет ручку, свой листок бумаги и старается успеть записать числа от 1 до 100 прежде, чем другому игроку удастся выбросить дубль. Первый, кому удалось это сделать, выигрывает.

队员投中两个一样的骰子可以拿起笔在卡片上从1向100写数字。第一个写到100的人胜出！

İki zarda aynı sayıyı tutturan oyuncular hemen kalemi ellerine alır ve kartlarının üzerine birden yüze kadar yazmaya başlarlar. Yüz sayısına ulaşabilen ilk kişi oyunu kazanır.

El jugador que logra lanzar doble, toma el único lápiz y escribe en su papel los números del 1 al 100. La primera persona en lograrlo es el ganador.

サイコロ2個を振って、同じ「字が出たらペンを受け取り、紙に1から100までの「字を書きます。次に同じ「字を出す人が現れるまで「字を書き「けることができ、最初に100まで書いた人が勝ちです。

Тоглогчид хосоороо нэгээс нэг зуу хүртэл тоог картан дээр балаар бичнэ. Нэг зуу хүргэсэн эхний хүн ялагч болно!

Il giocatore che tirando i dadi fa un numero doppio prende la biro e scrive sul suo cartoncino i numeri da uno a cento. La prima persona che riesce ad arrivare a cento vince.

Les joueurs qui roulent des doubles dés prennent le crayon et écrivent sur leur carton les chiffres de un à cent. La première personne à atteindre cent gagne!

שחקנים שמקבלים מספרים זהים (דאבל) בקוביות חוטפים את העט וכותבים על הכרטיס שלהם את המספרים מ-1 עד 100. הראשון שמגיע ל-100 מנצח!

Spelers die twee dezelfde dobbelstenen gooien, pakken de pen en schrijven de nummers van één tot honderd op hun kaart. De eerste persoon die de honderd haalt, wint!

Οι παίκτες που ρίχνουν διπλά αρπάζουν το στυλό και γράφουν στο χαρτί τους αριθμούς από το ένα έως το εκατό. Ο πρώτος που θα γράψει μέχρι το εκατό κερδίζει!

ผู้เล่นที่ ยนลกู เต๋า 2 ลูกู พรอ้ มกนั ออกมาได เ้ ลขตรงกนั ทงั้ สองลูก จะไดส้ ทิ ธหิ ยบิ ปากกามาเขยี นเลข 1-100ใคร เขยีนไดถ้ งึเลข100กอนจะเปนผชู้นะ

Sobald ein Mitspieler einen Pasch würfelt, rufen alle Mitspieler „Pasch" und der Mitspieler erhält den Stift. Während er auf seiner Karte beginnt, so schnell wie möglich die Zahlen von 1 bis 100 zu notieren, werden die zwei Würfel weiter gereicht. Wer als erstes die 100 erreicht, hat gewonnen.

Deltagerne som slår to ens med to terning, snupper kuglepennen og begynder at skrive tallene fra 1-100 på sit kort. Den første der når til 100 har vundet.

Jogadores que acertem em duplos ao lançar os dados, pegam na caneta e escrevem três números (de um a cem). A primeira pessoa a chegar aos 100 ganha!

168

41 Seven
A Counting Game Just For Fun

1, 2, 3, 4, 5, 6, CLAP, 8, 9...

Seven is a counting game with consequences. Begin in a small circle of people. One person begins the count and says aloud, "one." The next person says, "two," and the next, "three." The count continues like this, up to "six." Instead of the next person saying seven, they clap (which signifies the number seven and reverses the direction). The person who said "six" is now the next person in the sequence, and says, "eight," and the activity continues until the next multiple of seven (fourteen) or the next number with a seven in it (seventeen) is reached.

Anyone that makes a mistake (by saying the name of a multiple of seven or a number with seven in it instead of clapping) turns a 360 revolution while singing the "I'm Sorry" song.* And then the game resumes from the beginning, starting with "one."

* The I'm Sorry Song
*"I'm sorry, I blew it. I'm sorry, I knew it.
I'm really, really, really very sorry!"*

A small circle of people count from 1 to 50. Instead of saying the number seven (7), a multiple of seven (21), or any number with a seven in it (37), that person claps. Clapping also reverses the direction. First team to count to 50 without making a mistake, wins!

В небольшом кругу игроки по очереди считают от 1 до 50. Но вместо того, чтобы назвать цифру 7, или число кратное семи (например, 21), или любое число, в составе которого есть цифра 7 (например, 37), игрок хлопает в ладоши. После хлопка также сменяется направление движения. Первая команда, которой удается досчитать до 50 без ошибок, выигрывает.

一小圈人从1数到50。将与数字7或7的倍数有关的数字替换成拍手。拍手的同时反转方向。第一个准确数到50的小组胜出！

Halka halindeki küçük bir grup 1'den 50'ye kadar saymaya başlar. Kişi, yedi sayısını (7), yedinin katlarını (21), ya da içinde yedi geçen herhangi bir sayıyı (37) söylemek yerine sıra bu sayılara geldiğinde alkışlar. Alkış aynı zamanda sayma sırasının yönünü de değiştirir. Elliye kadar hatasız bir şekilde sayabilen ilk grup oyunu kazanır.

Un grupo pequeño de personas cuentan del 1 al 50. pero en vez de decir el 7, un múltiplo de 7 o cualquier número que tenga un 7, esa persona aplaude. Cuando aplaude se devuelve la dirección. El primer equipo en contar hasta 50 sin esquivocarse, GANA!

輪になって、順番に1から50まで「えます。ただし、7の倍「と7が含まれる「字のときは、「字を言わずに手を叩き、逆回「にして「え「けます。間違わずに最初に50まで「えることのできたチ「ムが勝ちです。

Цөөн хүнтэй тойрог үүсгэн нэгээс тавь хүртэл тоолно. Долоо (7) гэж хэлэхийн оронд долоогийн үржигдсэн тоог (21) юмуу эсвэл долоогийн тоо орсон аль нэг тоог (37) хэлсэн хүн алга ташина. Алга ташилт чиглэлийг өөрчилнө. Тавь хүртэл алдаа гаргалгүй тоолсон эхний баг ялагч болно!

In un piccolo cerchio, si conta da uno a cinquanta. Invece di dire il numero sette (7), un multiplo di sette (21), o qualsiasi numero che contenga il sette (37) si battono le mani. Battendo le mani si cambia anche la direzione di gioco. Il primo team che riesce a contare fino a cinquanta senza fare errori vince.

Un petit cercle de personnes compte de un à cinquante. Au lieu de dire le chiffre sept (7), un multiple de sept (21), ou n'importe quel chiffre qui contient un sept dedans (ex. 37), cette personne tape des mains. Taper des mains renverse aussi la direction. La première équipe à compte jusqu'à cinquante sans se tromper gagne!

מעגל קטן של אנשים סופר מ-1 ל-50. במקום להגיד את המספר 7, כפולה של 7 (21), או כל מספר שיש בו 7 (37), האדם שתורו הגיע מוחא כפיים. מחיאת כפיים גם הופכת את הכיוון. הקבוצה הראשונה שסופרת עד 50 בלי לטעות מנצחת.

In een kleine kring telt men van één tot vijftig. In plaats van het nummer zeven (7) te zeggen, of een meervoud van zeven (21), of enig nummer met een zeven in het getal (37) klapt de persoon die dan aan de beurt is zijn handen. Maar als men klapt, verandert de richting ook. Het team dat als eerste tot vijftig kan tellen zonder een fout te maken, wint!

Οι παίκτες ενός μικρού κύκλου μετρούν από το ένα έως το πενήντα, με τη σειρά, ένα νούμερο ο κάθε ένας. Αντί να πουν επτά (7), ένα παράγωγο του επτά (21) ή έναν αριθμό που να περιλαμβάνει το επτά (37), χτυπάνε παλαμάκια. Τα παλαμάκια αντιστρέφουν και τη φορά του μετρήματος. Η πρώτη ομάδα που θα μετρήσει μέχρι το πενήντα χωρίς να κάνει λάθος κερδίζει!

จับ กลุ่มเล็ก ๆ เป็นวงกลมแล้ว นับ 1-50 ขณ ขี อิ แมว้้ำแทนทวีธี ะออกเสีย งพดุ เมีอ นับถึง เลข 7 หรือ เมีอ ถึง เลขทดคี ณ ดว้ ย 7 อยา ง เช่น 21 หรือ ลงทา ยดว้ ย 7 อยา ง เช่น 37 ใหป้ รบมือ แทนการออกเสีย ง เมีอ มี ่ ครปรบมือ แล้ว ใหว้ ินผู้ เล่นยอ้นกลบัมาทมีใดนบัถึง50ก่อนเป็นผขู้ช้นะ

Zählt im Kreis von 1 bis 50. Bei jeder Zahl, die irgendwie mit 7 zu tun hat, also ein Vielfaches von 7 oder eine Zahl, die eine 7 enthält, klatscht der jeweilige Mitspieler in die Hände anstatt die Zahl zu nennen. Danach wird direkt in umgekehrter Richtung im Kreis weiter gezählt. Das Team, das als erstes fehlerfrei bis 50 kommt, hat gewonnen.

I en mindre cirkel tæller deltagerne fra 1-50. I stedet for at sige tallet (7) eller et tal, som kan divideres med 7 (7-tabellen f.eks. 21), eller numre med 7 i (37), klapper vedkommende. Klap ændrer også retning. Første hold, der tæller til 50 uden at lave fejl, har vundet.

Um pequeno círculo de pessoas contam até cinquenta. Em vez de dizer o número sete (7), um múltiplo de sete (21), ou qualquer número com um sete (37), têm de bater palmas. Mas bater palmas também muda o sentido. A primeira equipa a contar até cinquenta sem cometer um erro ganha!

One, Two, Three, Scream!

42 One, Two, Three, Scream!
A Small Circle Game Just For Fun

This no prop game incorporates two unusal components: strategy and screaming!

Begin with players standing in a small circle, and ask them to look down at their feet. When prompted to *look up*, each person is asked to stare directly at just one other player in the circle. If the person they are looking at also happens to be looking at them, both players scream. In the traditional version of the game, the first time you scream, you loose the use of one eye (which you cover up with one hand). Play continues, and if a one-eyed player screams again, they are out, and the circle shrinks until only one or two players remain.

If you like this game and would like to increase the energy (and noise level), try this variation: when two players look at each other, they scream, and the person who stops screaming first is out!

English Russian Chinese Turkish Spanish Japanese Mongolian Italian

Circles of people begin by looking down at their feet. When they look up, they stare at one other member of the group. If that person is also looking at them, both people scream!

В небольшом кругу игроки стоят, опустив глаза вниз. По команде они поднимают глаза и пристально смотрят на любого другого участника игры. Если случилось так, что игроки смотрят друг на друга, оба взвизгивают.

一小圈人首先低头看自己的脚。当他们抬头的时候盯着另一个成员，如果那个人也在看他们，两人同时尖叫。

Halka halindeki küçük bir grup oyuna ayaklarına bakarak başlarlar. Başlarını kaldırdıklarında başka bir grup elemanına gözlerini dikerler. Eğer o kişi de o anda onlara bakıyorsa, ikisi de çığlık atarlar.

En círculos de pocas personas, comienzan por mirar hacia el suelo, y cuando miran de frente, miran a una de las personas del círculo. Cuando dos personas conectan sus miradas, ambas gritan.

輪になり、下を向いて立ちます。指示に「って視線を上げたら、誰かの顔を見ます。目が合ったら、同時に叫びます。

Цөөн хүнтэй тойрог үүсгэж, оролцогчид өөрсдийн хөл рүү доош харна. Дээшээ харахдаа бүлгийн өөр нэг гишүүн рүү ширтэнэ. Хэрвээ тэр хүн тэдэн рүү харсан бол зэрэг хашгирна!

In piccoli gruppi, si comincia guardando verso il basso, guardandosi i piedi. Ad un certo punto si alza lo sguardo e si fissa un altra persona del team. Se anche l'altra persona ci sta fissando, tutti e due dobbiamo gridare!

174

Des petits cercles de personnes commencent en regardant leurs pieds. Lorsqu'ils lèvent les yeux, ils regardent une des personnes du groupe dans les yeux. Si cette même personne les regarde également, les deux personnes crient!

מעגלים קטנים של אנשים מתחילים בלהסתכל מטה על הרגליים שלהם. כאשר מרימים את הראש, מסתכלים על מישהו אחר בקבוצה. אם הבן הזה מסתכל עליו חזרה, שני האנשים צורחים!

In een kleine kring kijkt iedereen naar hun voeten. Als ze opkijken, maakt elk persoon contact met een andere persoon uit de kring. Als deze persoon ook naar de ander kijkt, schreeuwen beide mensen.

Οι παίκτες σε μικρές ομάδες σε κύκλο ξεκινούν κοιτώντας τα πόδια τους. Όταν κοιτάξουν πάνω, κοιτάζουν έντονα έναν άλλο παίκτη της ομάδας. Αν ο άλλος παίκτης τους κοιτάζει και αυτός, τότε και οι δύο ξεφωνίζουν δυνατά!

จับ กลุ่มกนั้ เล่ก ๆ เรมิ่ เล่นจากการกมั่ ลงมองที่ ทำ เมอื เงยหน้าขนึ มาใหเ ราเลอื กจอ่ งหน้าเฟอื่ ผูหนงึ่ คน ในกลุ่ม ถามคืนไหนเงยหน้ามาจอ้งตากนัพอดให้ทั้งคู่รอ้งกรดี!

Stellt Euch im Kreis auf und blickt auf Eure Füße. Schaut dann auf Kommando irgendeinen Mitspieler im Kreis an. Falls dieser Euch auch anschaut, schreit beide laut. Beim ersten Mal halten sich diese beiden Teilnehmer ein Auge zu, beim zweiten Schrei scheiden sie aus dem Kreis aus. Das Spiel endet, wenn sich nur noch ein oder zwei Teilnehmer im Kreis befinden.

I små cirkler af deltagere starter man med at kigge på egne fødder. Når der kigges op stirrer man på en anden person i gruppen. Hvis vedkommende stirrer på en, skriger begge to.

Em pequenos círculos, pessoas começam por olhar para os seus pés. Quando olham para cima, olham para outra pessoa. Se essa pessoa também olhar, as duas pessoas gritam!

43 Pencil Pushers

A Physical Game of Strength

This simple activity requires significant physical strength. Teams of four people push a pencil as far past a boundary line as they can. The only restriction is that the only part of their body that can touch the floor beyond the boundary line is their hands. Teams typically build some sort of human bridge, crawling over their teammates to push the pencil as far as they can.

Begin by creating a boundary line, using a rope, Raccoon Circle or sidewalk chalk. Provide each group with a single unsharpened pencil.

If any portion of a player's body touches the floor beyond the boundary line, that attempt is disqualified and the team is invited to try again. A successful team is able to build their human bridge, push the pencil as far as they can, and return all team members to the starting position without touching the floor beyond the boundary line with anything other than their hands.

Teams of four people try to push a pencil as far past a line as they can, with only their hands touching the space in front of the line.

Команды по 4 человека в каждой стараются бросить карандаш как можно дальше от линии. Единственное ограничение – непосредственно перед линией они могут опираться только на руки и ни на какие другие части тела.

四人一组，尝试将一支铅笔尽可能推离一条线，只有他们的手可以越过线前面的地方。

Dört kişilik gruplar halindeki takımlar çizginin önüne sadece elleri yere değecek şekilde bir kurşun kalemi itebildikleri kadar uzak bir çizgiye itmeye çalışırlar.

En equipos de 4 personas intentan de empujar un lápiz lo mas lejos posible despues de la raya, utilizando solo sus manos tocando el espacio delante de la raya.

4人組になって、鉛筆を境界線からどれだけ遠くに置くことができるかを競います。ただし、境界線から先は手しかついてはいけません。

Дөрвөн хүний бүрэлдэхүүнтэй багууд харандааг шугамын дагуу аль болох хол түлхэнэ, ингэхдээ гараа газраас хөндий байлгана.

Gruppi di quattro persone cercano di spingere una matita il più lontano possibile oltre una linea. Oltre la linea soltanto le mani possono toccare terra.

Des équipes de quatre personnes essaient de pousser un crayon le plus loin possible de la ligne. Seules leurs mains peuvent toucher l'espace devant la ligne.

קבוצות של ארבעה אנשים מנסות לדחוף עפרון הכי רחוק שאפשר מעבר לקו, כאשר רק הידיים נוגעות בשטח שמעבר לקו.

Teams van vier mensen proberen een potlood zover mogelijk als ze kunnen over een lijn te duwen. Echter mogen alleen hun handen de ruimte over de lijn raken.

Ομάδες των τεσσάρων ατόμων προσπαθούν να σπρώξουν ένα μολύβι πέρα από ένα όριο όσο πιο γρήγορα μπορούν, με μόνο τα χέρια τους να ακουμπούν στο έδαφος μπροστά από το όριο.

จับ กลุ่มกัน 4 คนช่วยกัน ดัน ปากกาใหผ้ ่านเส้น ฑูขี ดี ไวไ ห ไ กุลทสี่ ด โดยทอี นุญาตใหเ ฉพาะมอี เท่านนั้ ที แตะพนี ทลี าเส้น ได้

Versucht in Viererteams einen Bleistift so weit wie möglich von einer Startlinie aus in Richtung Ziel zu rollen. Dabei dürfen nur die Hände über die Startlinie hinaus reichen.

Grupper på 4 prøver at skubbe en blyant så langt over en linje som muligt. Kun deres hænder må røre området foran linjen.

Equipas de quatro pessoas tentam empurrar um lápis o mais longe de uma linha possível, apenas com as mãos a tocar o espaço após a linha.

180

44 Polar Bears & Ice Holes
A Guessing Game With Dice

You can have an ice hole without a polar bear, but you cannot have a polar bear without an ice hole.

For this game, the game leader has 4-8 dice in their hands. They shake the dice, open their hands and ask the group to observe the dice and then decide how many ice holes are present and how many polar bears.

The secret is: an ice hole is the center dot on the dice faces for 1, 3 and 5 and Polar bears are the dots around the center dots (two are present for the number 3, four are present for the number 5). Dice faces showing 2, 4 and 6 have no significance in this game.

In Kansas, they play a version called "Cowboys Around the Campfire" and you have to determine how many cowboys (dots around a central dot) are present.

English Players try to discover what features on dice are a polar bear or an ice hole.

Russian Игроки стараются догадаться, как на игральных кубиках определить количество лунок и белых медведей.

Chinese 队员尝试去发现骰子上北极熊或冰孔的特征是什么。

Turkish Oyuncular zarın üzerineki sayıların kutup ayısı mı yoksa buz deliği mi olduğunu bulmaya çalışır.

Spanish Los jugadores intentan descubrir las características de un dado, cuando son Oso Polar o un hueco de hielo?.

Japanese サイコロのどの目がホッキョクグマや氷の穴を示すかを｢てます。

Mongolian Тоглогчид шоон дээр цагаан баавгай юмуу мөсөн оромжийн аль нь байгаа болохыг олох.

Italian I giocatori cercano di indovinare quali elementi sui dadi sono orsi polari o buchi nel ghiaccio.

Les joueurs doivent découvrir ce qui figure sur les dés, soit un ours polaire ou un trou de glace.

שחקנים מנסים לגלות אלו צורות על הקוביה הם דוב קוטב או חור בקרח.

Spelers proberen erachter te komen welke eigenschappen op een dobbelsteen een ijsbeer voorstelt, of het hol van een ijsbeer.

Οι παίκτες προσπαθούν να ανακαλύψουν ποια χαρακτηριστικά στα ζάρια είναι πολική αρκούδα και ποια μια τρύπα στον πάγο.

ผู้ ล่นช่วยกนั คนั หาว่าลกู เต๋าจะออกหน้าให นทหี มายถงึ หมขี วั้ โลก หรอื หลุมน้ำแข็ง

Versucht heraus zu bekommen, wie man auf dem Würfel einen Eisbären oder ein Eisloch erkennt. Die Lösung nicht verraten, bis sie von allen gefunden wurde.

Medspillere prøver at finde ud af hvilken markering på en terning symboliserer en isbjørn eller et hul i isen.

Os jogadores tentam descobrir que faces do dado são ursos polares ou buracos no gelo.

45 The Virtual Slideshow
An Imaginary Picture Show

Invite the members of your group to close their eyes and remember the events of the day. Ask them to mentally take a photograph (or a video) of their favorite activity or moment. Then, when they have a photo in mind, open their eyes.

In order to allow other members of the group to 'see' these photographs, introduce the group to The Virtual Slideshow. You can provide a plastic 'clicker' device to make the clicking sound, or you can ask the group to make the sound of a slide projector or power point 'clicker' while lifting their hand (as if holding a remote control) and pointing it towards the location where their imaginary image will be visible. "Click!" Next, invite participants to show their imaginary image and to tell the group what is happening in this photo.

The Virtual Slideshow is an excellent way to encourage participants to share more information during a debriefing or reviewing session. Once they have a picture in mind, it is an easy task to talk about the content of the photo at length.

English

Share your favorite photographs of the day and describe what you see in each one. Use the clicker to forward to the next image.

Russian

Покажите друзьям воображаемую фотографию самого классного момента за сегодняшний день. Опишите каждую «фотографию». Пультом переключайтесь к следующей.

Chinese

分享你今天最喜欢的图像并描述每幅图像中你看到了什么。使用翻页器移到下一个图像。

Turkish

Günün en sevdiğiniz fotoğraflarını paylaşın ve her birinde ne gördüğünüzü tarif edin. Uzaktan kumanda kullanarak bir sonraki fotoğrafa geçin.

Spanish

Comparte tus fotografias favoritas del día, describiendo lo que vez en cada una de ellas. Usa un clicker para avanzar a la siguiente imágen.

Japanese

それぞれが思い浮かべるその日のお｢に入りの映像を共有するために、どのようなものが見えているかを｢明します。次の｢像に切り替えるサインとして、カチッと音のするものを用意します。

Mongolian

Тэр өдөр авсан өөрийнхөө хамгийн дуртай фото зургаа бусаддаа үзүүлэн тэдгээрт юу харснаа тодорхойл. Алсын удирдлага ашиглан дараагийн зургийг үзүүлнэ.

Italian

Condividi le tue foto preferite della giornata e descrivi cosa vedi in ciascuna di esse. Fai click con il telecomando per passare all'immagine successiva.

186

Partagez vos photos préférées de la journée et décrivez ce que vous voyez dans chacune. Utilisez le clic pour passer à la prochaine image.

שתף את הצילומים האהובים עליך מאותו יום, ותאר את מה שאתה רואה בכל תמונה. השתמש בשלט-רחוק כדי להתקדם לתמונה הבאה.

Deel je favoriete foto's van de dag met de groep en beschrijf wat je ziet in elke foto. Gebruik de klikker om de volgende foto te laten zien.

μοιραστείτε τις αγαπημένες σας φωτογραφίες της ημέρας και περιγράψτε το βλέπετε σε κάθε μία. Χρησιμοποιήστε το τηλεχειριστήριο για να περάσετε από τη μία φωτογραφία στην άλλη.

เอาภาพในความทรงจาทปี ระทบ ใจมาเล่าให้ พ่อี นๆ ฟัง โดยอธบิ ายใหท้ กุ คนเหน็ ภาพแลว้ ทาท่าคลกิ รีโมททเหมอืนว่าเล่อืนภาพเฟ่อืจะเล่าถึงภาพต่อไป

Beschreibe die für Dich wichtigsten und eindrücklichsten Momente des Tages so, als würden sie wie Fotografien in einer Diashow präsentiert. Nutze beim Wechseln von einem zum nächsten Foto einen Clicker oder eine virtuelle Fernbedienung.

Del dine favorit billede fra i dag og beskriv hvad du ser på billederne. Brug klikkeren for at klikke frem til det næste billede.

Partilhe as suas fotos favoritas do dia e descreva o que vê em cada uma delas. Utilize o comando para passar para a próxima imagem.

187

Here are several types of debriefing questions. You can find even more questions and techniques in the book *A Teachable Moment* (see page 220).

If you were to repeat this activity again, what would you do differently? Did each person in the group have the opportunity to contribute during the activity? If you were to hire a new employee to do this task, what skills would you want them to have? Would this activity have been easier with more or fewer people? What additional props or skills would have made this task easier? Did you spend more time planning or doing? List three things you will take away from this experience. What contributions did you make to the group? Which member of the group played a leadership role in this activity?

46 Debriefing Ball
The One Ball That Does It All

You'll need to write a dozen or more sequential numbers onto a ball with a permanent marker. Then toss this ball around the group. The person catching the ball identifies the number closest to their right thumb. A card filled with questions is produced and the person answers the question associated with the number they identified.

Question cards are prepared in advance and can be for a variety of topics, from leadership to teamwork to communication to debriefing or reviewing, such as: *What leadership talents do you find most helpful in a group setting?* or *How did you define sucess in this activity?* or *List three things that could have made your group more effective in this activity.* A spiral bound set of index cards is a simple way to keep track of your debriefing question cards.

189

Toss the ball. The catcher identifies the number closest to their right thumb and then answers the question associated with that number.

Бросьте мяч, на поверхности которого вы заранее написали несколько цифр. Тот, кто поймал мяч, определяет какая цифра ближе всего к большому пальцу его правой руки и отвечает на вопрос, заготовленный под этим номером.

投球。接到球的人确定离他右手拇指最近的数字，并回答该数字所对应的问题。

Topu atın. Topu yakalayan sağ başparmağına en yakın numarayı tanımlasın ve o numaraya sahip olan soruyu yanıtlasın.

Pasando la pelota. El que la ataja identifica el número mas cercano a su dedo gordo derecho y contesta la pregunta asociada a ese número.

「字を書いたボ」ルを投げます。ボ」ルを受けとめた人は、右の親指のいちばん近くにある「字にあらかじめ割り「てられた質問に答えます。

Бөмбөг шидэх. Бөмбөг баригч баруун гарынхаа эрхий хуруунд хамгийн ойр байгаа тоог тогтоож тэр тоотой холбоотой асуултанд хариулна.

Lancia la palla. Chi la riceve identifica il numero più vicino al suo pollice destro e quindi risponde alla domanda associata a questo numero.

190

Lancez le ballon. Celui qui l'attrape trouve le numéro le plus près de son pouce droit et répond ensuite à la question associée à ce numéro.

זרקו את הכדור. התופס מזהה את המספר הקרוב ביותר לאגודל יד ימין ועונה על השאלה של מספר זה.

Gooi de bal. Degene die de bal vangt, leest het nummer op de bal welke het dichtst bij zijn rechterduim is. Daarna beantwoordt hij de vraag die bij dat nummer hoort.

πετάξτε την μπάλα. Αυτός που την πιάνει λέει τον αριθμό που βρίσκεται πιο κοντά στον αντίχειρά του και μετά απαντά στην ερώτηση που σχετίζεται με αυτόν τον αριθμό.

โยนลูก บอลขนี้ คนทรี ปู้ ลกู บอลจะต้องแจ้ง หมายเลขทปี รากฏอยู่ใ กลนั้ วิ โป้งขา งขวาของตนเอง จากนนั้ใหต้อบคา ถามตามจานวนทตีวิเลขปรากฏขนึ้มา

Wirf den Fragen-Ball einem beliebigen Mitspieler zu. Der Fänger nimmt die Zahl, die seinem rechten Daumen am nächsten ist, und beantwortet die dieser Zahl zugeordneten Frage. Dann wirft er den Ball dem nächsten Mitspieler zu.

Kast bolden. Den som griber bolden siger det tal, der er tættest på deres højre tommelfinger og svarer på det spørgsmål, der er forbundet med dette nummer.

Atire a bola. Quem a apanhar identifica o número mais perto do seu polegar direito e de seguida responde à questão associada ao número.

French Hebrew Dutch Greek Thai. German Danish Portuguese

191

A Circle of Connection

47 A Circle of Connection
A Closing Activity

*Things which connect us bring
us a little bit closer together.*

Here is one of my favorite closing activities. One member of the group begins by introducing themselves to the group and standing with their hands on their hips, elbows out. This person mentions specific things they enjoyed about the program or event. The first person in the group who agrees with them links elbows with them. This second person then continues to mention significant things they enjoyed, and another person links to them. The activity continues until all members of the group have 'linked together.' The final task is for the last person to continue sharing until the first person can link to them, at which point everyone in the group will be standing connected in a small circle.

Players share their favorite elements of the program. Another player can connect (join elbows) with them if they agree. Play continues until everyone is connected in a circle.

Первый участник рассказывает о своих любимых элементах программы. Другой участник, услышав что-то близкое для себя, присоединяется к предыдущему, взяв его под руку. Игра продолжается, пока все участники не объединятся в единый круг.

队员分享他们在活动中最喜欢的部分。另一位队员如果同意可以与他连接起来（手挽手）。 游戏继续直到所有人连成一个圆圈。

Oyuncular programın en beğendikleri kısımlarını paylaşırlar. Diğer bir oyuncu öbür oyuncularla aynı şekilde düşünüyorsa (koluna girerek) onlara katılır. Oyun herkes birbirine kolkola bağlanana kadar devam eder.

Los jugadores comparten los elementos favoritos del taller. Un jugador puede conectarse (uniendo los codos) con los demás si estan de acuerdo. El juego continúa hasta que todos quedan conectados.

一人がプログラムの中で「しかったことを「表し、その「容に同意する人が「表者と腕を組みます。全員が腕を組み輪になるまで「けます。

Тоглогчид хөтөлбөр дэх өөрсдийн хамгийн дуртай дугаарыг бусадтайгаа хуваалцана. Өөр нэг тоглогч түүнийг зөвшөөрч байвал тохойгоо нийлүүлнэ. Тойрогт байгаа хүн бүр холбогдох хүртэл тоглоно.

I giocatori condividono i loro elementi preferiti del programma. Chi è d'accordo può connettersi con loro (unisce i gomiti). Il gioco continua fino a quando tutti sono connessi in un cerchio.

Les joueurs discutent de l'élément qu'ils ont préféré du programme de la journée. Un autre joueur peut s'y joindre coude à coude s'il est d'accord. Le jeu se poursuit jusqu'à ce que tout le monde soit relié en cercle.

שחקן משתף את הקבוצה בחלק האהוב עליו בתכנית. שחקן אחר יכול
להתחבר אליו (משלבים מרפקים) אם הוא מסכים. ממשיכים לשחק עד
שכולם מחוברים במעגל.

Deelnemers vertellen hun favoriete elementen van een programma. Als een andere deelnemer het hiermee eens is, gaat hij arm in arm staan met degene die spreekt. Deze deelnemer vertelt dan zijn favoriete element, enzovoorts. Ga door totdat iedereen in de groep deel uit maakt van de kring.

Οι παίκτες μιλάνε για τα αγαπημένα τους σημεία στο πρόγραμμα. Οι άλλοι παίκτες ενώνουν τους αγκώνες τους με αυτόν που μιλάει, αν συμφωνούν με αυτά που λέει. Το παιχνίδι συνεχίζεται μέχρι να ενωθούν όλοι οι παίκτες.

ผู้ เล่นคนแรกยนี่ เท่า เอวไว้ แล้วบ๊ บอกถงี่ ช่วงหรอี่ เหตุการณ์ทดี นเอง ชอบมากจากกจิ กรรมอบูรมรมครงั้ นี้ หากเพอื่นคนไหนเหน็ด้วยหรอี่สู้กคิ เหมอืนกนันักให้มายนี้เทาเอวชนขอ้ศอกตอ่ๆกนไปไปเล่นไปเรอื่ยๆจนกว่า ทุกคนจะเหน็ ด้วยในขอ้ต่างๆจนสามารถต่อกนันี้เป็นวงกลมได้ทงั้หมด

Ein Teilnehmer beginnt und zählt laut auf, was ihm an der Veranstaltung am besten gefallen hat. Wenn ein anderer Teilnehmer einem der genannten Punkte zustimmt, stellt er sich so neben den ersten Teilnehmer, dass er dessen Ellenbogen berührt. Er zählt nun seinerseits seine Highlights auf, und ein weiterer Teilnehmer stellt sich Ellbogen an Ellbogen neben ihn und übernimmt die Aufzählung. So läuft die Rückmeldungsrunde, bis die beiden letzten Teilnehmer eine Gemeinsamkeit entdecken und der Kreis geschlossen ist.

En deltager fortæller, hvad de synes bedst om i forhold til programmet. En anden deltager låser arm med vedkommende (arm i arm), hvis de er enige og fortsætter fortællingen. Legen fortsætter, indtil alle er en del af cirklen.

Os jogadores partilham os seus elementos favoritos do programa. Outro jogador pode conectar (juntar cotovelos) com a pessoa, se concordar. O jogo continua até que todas as pessoas no circulo estiverem conectadas.

Thumbprints

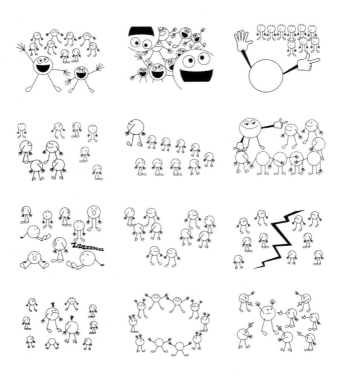

These debriefing images are from the
Teamwork & Teamplay Training Cards
and were created by Dave Knobbe.

48 Thumbprints
Debriefing Images

The twelve thumbprints in the Teamwork & Teamplay Training Cards (and also shown on the previous page) illustrate a variety of team performance situations. Place these images so that they are visible to your group. Then invite participants to interact with these images while discussing the following questions:

1. Place these images in order from best (ideal) team behavior to worst (poorest team behavior).

2. Which images illustrate positive team behavior and which are negative?

3. Which image most accurately illustrates the present nature of this group right now?

4. Which image is most like this group when things are going well? Which image represents this group under pressure or experiencing conflict?

5. Which thumbprint (circle person) do you most identify with in any given illustration? Why?

Which of the group performance images best reflects your team?

Какая из картинок лучше всего представляет вашу команду?

哪一组团队表现的图像可以最好地反映你的团队?

Grubun performans resimlerinden hangisi sizin takımınızı en iyi şekilde yansıtır?

Cuál de este grupo de imágenes representa mejor el desempeño de tu equipo?

グル「プの「きを示すイメ「ジのうち、あなたのチ「ムの「況をもっとも表しているのはどれでしょう?

Бүлгийн гүйцэтгэлийн хэлбэрүүдээс аль нь таны мөрөөдлийг тусган харуулж байна вэ?

Quale delle immagini sulla performance del gruppo rappresenta meglio il vostro team?

Laquelle des images de performance de groupe reflète le mieux votre équipe?

איזה מהתמונות של ביצועים קבוצתיים הכי משקפת את הקבוצה שלך?

Welke van de foto's van de groepsprestatie geeft de beste reflectie weer van jouw team?

Ποιες από τις εικόνες απόδοσης της ομάδας καλύτερα αντικατοπτρίζουν την ομάδα σας;

ภาพของกลุ่มไหนออกมาดที่ สี ̖ดแสดงถงึ ประะ สทิ ธภิ าพการทางานรว่ มกนั ของทมี

Welches Sinnbild stellt am ehesten die Gruppenleistung Deines Teams dar?

Hvilket af teamwork billederne afspejler bedst dit team?

Que imagem melhor reflecte o seu grupo?

For even more games and circle activities with
Raccoon Circles, see *The Revised and Expanded
Book of Raccoon Circles* or download the
free internet edition of Raccoon Circles at:
www.teamworkandteamplay.com

49 The Final Transmission
A Closing Activity With Movement

Multiple groups of eight people each hold a knotted Raccoon Circle with their left hand and begin to walk forward (like a giant gear turning in space). Nearby circles are also turning, and the members of each group can high five each other as they pass. You can add music (or singing) to this closing activity and think of it as a way for many people to connect during the final activity of the day. You can also change directions and have groups change location within the available space.

Multiple small groups holding a rope circle rotate (like gears) and high-five each other as they pass.

Множество небольших групп, держась левой рукой за канат, который объединяет их в круги, перемещаются по залу, как гигантские механизмы. Встретившись с другими, участники правой рукой дают «пять» друг другу.

多个小组拉着绳子旋转（像齿轮一样），
与和他们经过的人击掌。

Halat halkayı tutan çeşitli küçük gruplar (çark gibi) dönerler ve geçtikçe birbirlerine "çak hareketi" yaparlar.

En muchos grupos pequeños, agarrados de una cinta o cuerda amarrada en círculo, van rotando como engranajes y cada vez que coinciden con una persona de otro círculo, chocan las manos.

小さなグル「プごとにロ「プでつくった輪っかを左手で持ち、回「しながらほかのグル「プのメンバ「とハイタッチをして、ギアがかみ合うような動きをします。

Цөөн хүнтэй олон бүлгүүд олс барин араа мэт тойргийг үүсгэн эргэлдэнэ, ингэж эргэлдэж, зөрж ойртох үедээ алгаа нийлүүлэн цохино.

Tanti piccoli gruppi - che tengono con una mano un cerchio di corda al centro - ruotano su se stessi (come ingranaggi) e "battono il cinque" ai gruppi vicini mentre passano.

Plusieurs petits groupes, qui tiennent chacun une cercle de corde, font une rotation (comme un mécanisme) et se tapent haut la main en se croisant.

הרבה קבוצות קטנות שמחזיקות טבעת חבל מסתובבים (כמו גלגלי-שיניים) ונותנים כיף אחד לשני כאשר חולפים זה ליד זה.

Meerdere kleine groepen houden een touw vast met één hand en draaien in een cirkel. Als ze langs leden van andere groepen lopen, geven ze elkaar een high five.

Πολλαπλές μικρές ομάδες κρατάνε ένα σκοινί δεμένο σε κύκλο και περιστρέφονται χτυπώντας χέρια στον αέρα καθώς συναντάνε παίκτες από άλλους κύκλους.

จบั กลุ่มเป็นวงเลก็ ๆ หลายๆกลุ่ม หลายๆวง แล้ว้ เคล่อื นตวั แบบหมนุ วงลอ่ เหมอื นฟันเฟือง เมอื หมนุ ผ่านกลุ่มไหนกใ็หแตะมอืไฮไฟวก์นั

6-8 Mitspieler bilden eine Kreisgruppe, in dem sie sich mit der linken Hand an einem zum Kreis geknoteten Seil festhalten. Die Gruppen rotieren wie Zahnräder zueinander, in dem die einzelnen Gruppenmitglieder die Mitglieder anderer Kreise beim gegenläufigen Gehen einander auf die rechte Hand abklatschen.

I flere små grupper holdes der en rebcirkel mellem deltagerne og rebcirklerne roteres som et tandhjul. Giv "high five" til andre gruppemedlemmer, når de passerer hinanden.

Múltiplos pequenos grupos seguram uma corda em circulo e rodam (como engrenagens) e dão um "high-five" à medida que passam.

203

50 Shuffle Left / Shuffle Right
An Active Reviewing Technique With Movement

At the completion of an activity, invite your group to stand in a circle (around the location of the now completed activity and equipment) and instruct them how to perform this kinesthetic debriefing technique.

Begin by asking participants to shuffle (step sideways) to the left (clockwise) around the circle. This motion continues until someone in the group says, 'stop,' and presents to the group their thoughts about the recent activity or a more specific question framed by the facilitator (such as: what skills did you need to accomplish the last activity?). When finished, the speaker says, "shuffle left,' or 'shuffle right,' and the circle rotates again until another person says stop.

If at any time during this activity the group makes an entire 360 degree rotation of the circle without anyone saying stop, it is time to move on to the next activity.

Shuffle Left / Shuffle Right will keep your group in motion and provide the opportunity for even the quietest voice to be heard.

As a reviewing technique, share your thoughts and then circle right or left until someone else says 'stop' and shares their thoughts.

В качестве анализа поделитесь своими мыслями с другими участниками, а затем меняйтесь местами с соседями справа и слева по кругу, пока кто-то еще не скажет «стоп» и не поделится своими мыслями.

作为一个回顾技巧，分享你的想法并指示向右转圈或向左转圈，直到有人喊"停"后接着分享他们的想法。

Değerlendirme tekniği olarak, fikirlerinizi paylaşın ve sonra biri tekrar "dur" diyene kadar sağa ya da sola dönün.

Como una técnica de revisión, comparta sus impresiones y luego circule a la derecha o izquierda hasta que otra persona dice Stop y comparte sus impresiones.

ふりかえりの手法として、自分の考えを話した後に、右回﹁か左回﹁かを指示し、誰かが「ストップ」というまで回﹁します。「ストップ」と言った人は、次に自分の考えを話します。

Сүүлчийн тоглоом учраас та өөрийн санал бодлоо хуваалцаж хэн нэг нь "зогс" гэж хэлээд өөрийнхөө бодлыг хуваалцаж эхлэх хүртэл баруун юмуу зүүн тийш эргэлдэнэ.

Una tecnica di riflessione sull'esperienza. Condividi i tuoi pensieri, poi il gruppo ruota verso destra o verso sinistra fino a quando qualcuno dice "stop" e condivide i propri pensieri.

Une activité de révision. Partagez vos commentaires puis tournez à droite ou à gauche jusqu'à ce que quelqu'un demande d'arrêter pour partager ses commentaires.

כטכניקת סיכום, שתף את הקבוצה במחשבותיך, ואז הסתובבו במעגל לימין או לשמאל עד שמישהו אחר אומר "עצור" ומשתף את המחשבות שלו.

Om terug te blikken op een activiteit of het gehele programma, deel je gedachten met de groep. Geef dan aan of de groep links of rechts draait in de cirkel. De groep loopt door totdat iemand anders "stop" zegt en zijn gedachten deelt.

Σαν μια τεχνική ανασκόπησης, μοιραστείτε τις σκέψεις σας και μετά όλη η ομάδα περιστρέφεται, μέχρι κάποιος να πει στοπ, οπότε και είναι έτοιμος να μοιραστεί με τη σειρά του τις σκέψεις του.

ทาตามเทคนิค โดยจบ กลุ่มเป็นวงกลมแล้ว หัน ขวา หัน ซ้า ย ไป เรื่อ ยๆจนมุมคี นพูดว่า "หยุด " คนนนนั้ จะ มีโอกาสแสดงความคดิ เหนิ และสงให้หันขวาหันซ้ายสลบไปมาได้

Teilt Eure Gedanken, Erfahrungen und Einsichten zum Tag in einer Feedbackrunde. Ihr bewegt Euch dazu im Kreis entweder rechts oder links herum bis jemand „Halt!" sagt. Derjenige, der halt gesagt hat, formuliert dann in wenigen Sätzen sein Feedback zur Veranstaltung. Danach sagt er „rechts herum" oder „links herum". Die Gruppe geht gemäß seiner Anweisung weiter, bis der nächste „Halt!" sagt und sein Feedback gibt.

Som en refleksions teknik, del dine tanker og fortsæt så med at gå til højre eller venstre i cirklen indtil én siger "stop" og deler deres tanker.

Como técnica de revisão, partilhe os seus pensamentos e de seguida circule para a direita ou para a esquerda até que alguém diz "stop" e partilhe os seus pensamentos.

Pillow Talk Questions

What challenged you today? How far did you hike today? How many different kinds of food did you taste today? What was your favorite moment of the day? Did you make a new friend today? What was your favorite activity today? What groups were you a part of today? What staff member encouraged you today? What did you discover today? What did you learn today? Who did you meet today? Did you create anything today? What part of today would you like to repeat again? What was your favorite song (or dance) today? Did you see any animals today? Describe the sunrise or sunset today. Describe today in just one word. What surprised you today?

51 Pillow Talk
A Wonderful Way to End the Day

Here is a unique and powerful activity for the end of a day. This activity works well if you have access to the sleeping areas of your program participants. During the evening hours, while your participants are busy with other activities, visit the sleeping area (cabin, tent, bedroom) and secretly place a question card beneath the pillow of each participant. At night, just before bedtime, invite your participants to find the card below their pillow, read the question presented there and reflect on their day.

Pillow Talk cards should focus on questions which bring up positive images from the day. By focusing on a positive event, the final waking moments of your participants will be happy ones. Participants can reflect individually on the question presented on their card, or they can share their thoughts with others in the room.

Secretly hide a question card below the sleeping pillow of each group member. At night, invite each person to find and then answer the question on their card.

Когда никто не видит, спрячьте под подушкой каждого карточку с неким вопросом. Перед сном попросите посмотреть под подушкой и ответить на свой вопрос.

在每个人的枕头下藏一张问题卡片，晚上邀请大家找到这张问题卡片并回答上面的问题。

Grubun her elemanın yastığının altına gizlice bir soru kartı saklayın. Gece, her bir elemanın soru kartını bulup cevap vermesi için bu oyuna davet edin.

Muy discretamente esconda una tarjeta con una pregunta debajo de la almohada de cada participante. En la noche, invite a cada participante a buscar su pregunta y contestarla.

キャンパ「の枕の下にこっそりと質問カ「ド を「しておきます。「る前に、カ「ドに書かれ た質問に答えるように促します。

Бүлгийн гишүүн бүрийн дэрэн доор асуултын картыг нууна. Шөнө тэр асуултыг хайж олоод түүнд хариулахад уриална.

Senza farti vedere, nascondi un cartoncino con una domanda sotto al cuscino di ogni membro del gruppo. Di notte, invita ciascuno a trovare il suo cartoncino e poi a rispondere alla domanda.

En cachette, dissimulez une carte de question sous l'oreiller de chaque membre du groupe. Le soir venu, invitez chaque personne à la trouver et puis à répondre à la question sur leur carte.

החביאו בסתר כרטיס עם שאלה מתחת לכרית במיטה של כל חבר בקבוצה. בלילה, הזמינו את המשתתפים למצוא את הכרטיס ולענות על השאלה.

Verstop een kaartje met daarop een vraag onder het kussen van ieder lid van de groep. 's Avonds, nodig ieder persoon uit om dit kaartje te vinden en de vraag op zijn kaartje te beantwoorden.

Κρύψτε μια κάρτα με ερώτηση κάτω από το μαξιλάρι του κάθε μέλους μιας ομάδας. Το βράδυ καλέστε κάθε παίκτη να βρει και μετά να απαντήσει την ερώτηση στην κάρτα του.

แอบเอาการ์ด คาถูามไปวางไว้ใต้ หมอน มอนุของเพ่อี ในในกลุ่ม พอตอนค่า บอกใหเ พ่อี นไปหาการ์ด นนั้ และ ตอบคาถาม บนการ์ด

Platziere unbemerkt im Laufe des Tages eine Karte mit einer Frage unter dem Kopfkissen eines jeden Gruppenmitglieds. Lade am Abend die Teilnehmer ein, die Frage auf der Karte für sich zu beantworten.

I al hemmelighed gemmes et kort under hver deltagers hovedpude. Til aften inviteres alle til at finde kortet og svare på spørgsmålet på deres kort.

Discretamente esconda um cartão com uma pergunta por debaixo da almofada de cada membro do grupo. Á noite convide cada pessoa a procurar e a responder a pergunta do cartão.

Equipment for Teamwork & Teamplay

The activities in this book were chosen to minimize the amount of equipment required, especially for regions of the world where such equipment can be difficult to find. Here is a list of the unique equipment mentioned in this book. The hardware for each of these teambuilding props can be purchased locally or from the T&T equipment supplier, Training Wheels, Inc. (www.training-wheels.com or 1-888-553-0147).

Raccoon Circles are 15 foot (4.5 meter) long segments of 1" (25.4mm) wide tubular climbing webbing. You can also use rope, string or even shoelaces for many Raccoon Circle activities.

Bull Rings are 1.5" (38mm) diameter welded harness (metal) rings. These rings will easily carry a tennis or golf ball. Attach 10-12 strings. You can also use a keyring, shower curtain ring or plastic tube.

Fishhooks are made from a wooden alphabet block (pine), with six holes drilled completely through. After passing six strings through these holes, nearby strings are knotted together and then six different metal hardware hooks are attached. Add hooks to some additional wood blocks for stacking, or for a higher challenge, try to pick up a mousetrap without setting it off.

Petecas are a hand version of hacky sack, created in Brazil and played all over the world. You can find an extensive document with instructions for making your own Peteca (featherball) at the T&T website.

The **Debriefing Ball** is made from a soccer ball or playground ball. A permanent marker is used to draw letters or numbers on the surface of the ball.

Thumbprints are the creation of David Knobbe and are team behavior images that you can use for reviewing sessions at the completion of a program. A collection of twelve of these images is included in each deck of Teamwork & Teamplay Training Cards.

Magic Carpets are made from tough vinyl (plastic) sheets roughly 6 ft. x 6 ft. (2 x 2 meters). A plastic tablecloth, tarp or shower curtain can also be used. These same items can also be used for the activities Team Tarp Jump and Sunny Side Up.

Match Cards are a collection of 24 cards (twelve pairs of matching images or words) made from index cards or cardboard. There are two decks of 24 match cards in each deck of T&T training cards.

The **Virtual Slideshow Clicker** is actually a dog training device that can be found at most pet stores. The sound of this clicker is similar to the sound of an old-fashioned 35mm slide projector as it advances to the next slide.

If you would like to find a regional supplier for Teamwork & Teamplay books and equipment, here are a few organizations that carry T&T gear:

Worldwide Training Wheels, Inc. CO, USA
www.training-wheels.com   888-553-0147

United States Trainer's Warehouse MA, USA
www.trainerswarehouse.com   800-299-3770

Canada Adventureworks! Ontario, Canada
www.adventureworks.org   905-304-5683

Singapore Innotrek Singapore
www.innotrek.sg   +65 9002 8901

China China Camp Association Beijing, China
www.weibo.com/CCAorg   400-890-9151

England RSVP Design United Kingdom
www.rsvp.co.uk   +44 141 561 038

Germany Metalog Germany
www.metalog.de   +49 (0) 8142 / 4411 400

The Pangaia Project
A Conversation with Dr. Jim Cain

When my publisher first mentioned to me that a significant number of my books were being purchased overseas, I was surprised and excited. I was also informed by my web programmer that traffic to my website came from over one hundred different countries. Suddenly I was presented with the possibilities that my contributions could benefit not just my own country, but many other countries in the world. Since that time, I've traveled to over thirty countries. I even had to add additional pages to my passport to allow space for future travels. All of these things contributed to my decision to create something that would truly be a global project. But at the outset, it was clear that language would be a challenge. How could I share the best of what I know in a manner that would eliminate language and cultural barriers?

The answer is this first collection of international translations for my favorite Teamwork & Teamplay activities. Thanks to the many friends and colleagues I've met over the years (many of whom are associated with the International Camping Fellowship), I had a capable pool of people willing to translate my words into the language of their own country.

I think of The Pangaia Project as my personal international diplomacy project. While most international diplomacy takes place at high levels between the governments of different countries, I wanted to create my own program. Something that would benefit facilitators, teachers, trainers, camp counselors and group leaders of all kinds, around the world. Here are a few of my thoughts about The Pangaia Project. You can find even more at my website (www.teamworkandteamplay.com).

I chose the Greek spelling of Pangaia rather than a more North American version because I hope this project will appeal to people around the world.

For this publication, I have selected activities that I consider the best of the best. Activities that create wonderful teachable moments for topics ranging from communication to leadership, building trust to building community and of course teamwork and teamplay. I chose teambuilding challenges, icebreakers, games and active reviewing techniques that have been valued in different cultures and countries. In order for an activity to be included here, it needs to 'work' in other cultures and countries. I also refined my original list of 100+ activities by choosing only those activities for which the necessary supplies and equipment are easily available in any part of the world. Simple props like rope, balls, pens and tarps can be found almost everywhere in the world, and many of the activities in this book require no equipment at all.

The languages represented in this first collection are largely based upon the nationalities of the friends and colleagues that volunteered to assist me. In the future, I would love to publish a second edition with other languages, including Native American, First Nation and other aboriginal languages. I welcome your suggestions and recommendations (especially if you are willing to help translate into your language). Contact me at: jimcain@teamworkandteamplay.com.

Pangaia is the name of the original supercontinent before the plates of our earth drifted apart from each other. This 'one world' is how our earth began. It may be a small contribution indeed, but I hope this collection of activities that build unity, community, connection and teamwork will bring all the people of the world just a little bit closer together.

If you enjoy this collection of Teamwork & Teamplay activities, you'll find additional activities in my other books. For a list of my books see page 220 and for even more information visit the T&T website at:

www.teamworkandteamplay.com

Pangaia Project Partners

This publication would not have been possible without the friends, colleagues, camp professionals and youth development specialists around the world that generously gave their time and efforts to translate my words and ideas into the language of their own country. I am eternally grateful to each person mentioned here and proud to call them my friends.

Russian Xenia Bejenar, Camp Industry
Chinese Ann Li, China Camp Association
Turkish Dr. Haluk Zulfikar & Dr. Ergül Berber
Spanish Carole Bosch, Campamento Hiawatha
Japanese Masako Harigaya, Tatsuya Kanayama, National Camping Association of Japan
Mongolian Mrs. Chultem Byambasuren, Mongolian Camping Association
Italian Guido Cremonesi, Landscape Training
French Association des Camps du Québec
Hebrew The Staff of Camp Stone
Dutch Ester Hoefsloot & Monique Klein Swormink
Greek Alexia Sideri, Delphi Camp
Thai Dr. Panwasa Katherine Smith, Windsor WEC
German Peter Jotzo and Alexandra Just
Danish Bent Sten Jensen, University of Copenhagen
Portuguese Miguel Ludwick, Projecto Novas Descobertas, Associacão Educativa e Recreativa

The International Camping Fellowship

The International Camping Fellowship is a worldwide assembly of camp and youth development professionals who gather together to share their enthusiasm, knowledge and commitment to the power of the camp experience.

The organization was founded in 1987 with the energy of camp professionals sharing the dream of a "better world through camping". The International Camping Fellowship welcomes all who foster international understanding through the organized camp experience.

The ICF has nearly 4000 members and affiliates in 80 countries. Additional information about the International Camping Fellowship can be found at: www.campingfellowship.org

ICf INTERNATIONAL CAMPING FELLOWSHIP

References & Resources

Additional Books by Jim Cain

Teamwork & Teamplay, Cain & Jolliff, ISBN 978-0-7872-4532-0. 417 award winning pages, considered by many to be 'the essential' teambuilding text.

Essential Staff Training Activities, Cain, Hannon & Knobbe, ISBN 978-0-7575-6167-2. Make your staff training active, engaging, memorable & fun!

A Teachable Moment – A Facilitator's Guide to Activities for Processing, Debriefing, Reviewing and Reflection, Cain, Cummings & Stanchfield, ISBN 978-0-7575-1782-2. 130 processing, debriefing & reviewing techniques for every group facilitator.

The Revised and Expanded Book of Raccoon Circles, Cain & Smith, ISBN 978-0-7575-3265-8. Hundreds of activities with one piece of webbing.

Teambuilding Puzzles, Cain, Cavert, Anderson & Heck, ISBN 978-0-7575-7040-7. 100 puzzles for teams that build valuable life skills.

400 Index Cards Jim Cain, Available in 2017. 100+ activities that you can create yourself with just index cards. For teachers, trainers, facilitators and group leaders of all kinds. Do more with less!

The Big Book of Low-Cost Training Games, Cain & Scannell, ISBN 978-0-07-177437-6. Effective activities that explore valuable training topics.

Find Something To Do! Jim Cain, ISBN 978-0-9882046-0-7 Jim's favorite collection of powerful activities with no equipment at all. Easy as 1-2-3!

Rope Games Jim Cain, ISBN 978-0-9882046-1-4 Create an infinite variety of group experiences with a finite collection of ropes.

T&T Training Cards Jim Cain, ISBN 978-0-9882046-2-1 Facilitate 17+ teambuilding activities with this unique deck of 65 large format cards. With instructions.

Teamwork & Teamplay - International Edition Jim Cain, ISBN 978-0-9882046-3-8 Fifty Team Activities, Sixteen Languages, One World!

You can find more information about these books at TeamworkandTeamplay.com, Amazon.com, KendallHunt.com and Training-Wheels.com.

You can find additional teambuilding activities, games and group building ideas (and much more!) at the Teamwork & Teamplay website:

www.teamworkandteamplay.com

A Special Thanks to Markel

Markel is excited to once again partner with
Dr. Jim Cain on his new initiative, the
Teamwork & Teamplay International Edition.

As a successful innovator in the camp and youth recreation insurance industry, Markel encourages the positive and fun tactics that this book delivers. How might you engage and entertain children with a few simple games or activities while waiting out a thunderstorm, when the bus breaks down, or if a parent is late for pick-up? The activities in this book provide a positive and fun way to manage circumstances safely—something Markel greatly encourages.

We hope the **Teamwork & Teamplay International Edition** provides many fun experiences and enhances your leadership toolbox with the ability to do dozens of new and unique games and activities.

To learn more about Markel, please visit
markelinsurance.com.

About Jim Cain

Dr. Jim Cain is the author of fifteen team and community building texts, including his classic first book, Teamwork & Teamplay. He has collected, improvised, researched and created hundreds of activities that build unity, community, connection, leadership and teamwork, and shared them with audiences around the world.

This international translation of T&T activities is the first publication of The Pangaia Project and with your help, there will be more.

Visit the Teamwork & Teamplay website for more information about Jim's books, teambuilding equipment, The Pangaia Project and other useful team and community building ideas.

If you would like to invite Jim to make a presentation at your next conference, workshop, training event or program, contact him at:

Jim Cain, Ph.D.
Teamwork & Teamplay
468 Salmon Creek Road
Brockport, New York 14420-9761 USA
Telephone 585-637-0328
Email: jimcain@teamworkandteamplay.com
Website: www.teamworkandteamplay.com

Thank you for reading the

Teamwork & Teamplay
International Edition

If you would like to obtain additional copies of this book or other books by Jim Cain, or invite Jim to speak at your next conference, workshop, staff training event or program, contact him at:

Jim Cain, Ph.D.

Teamwork & Teamplay

468 Salmon Creek Road
Brockport, New York 14420-9761 USA

Telephone 585-637-0328

Email: jimcain@teamworkandteamplay.com

Website: www.teamworkandteamplay.com